DEATH OF A DOVE

I have mixed fact and fiction in this story. The musical "To-nights the Night" was performed at the Gaiety Theatre in 1915. where it had 460 performances. Previously, in1914, the musical produced by George Grosssmith Jr. was performed in New York at the Shubert Theatre. A bomb from a Zeppelin hit the Dolphin Tavern in Red Lion Square and three were killed. The clock which stopped that day can still be viewed at the pub. A bomb fell near the Aldwych theatre, killing a boy who worked there. My father fought (Northants Reg) as a young officer at the battles of Mons and Ypres and nearly lost his leg from gangrene. Pelham is a family name and my grandmother was a Drummond.

To Julie
with best luck

Andrew Giffen

By the same author:

DEATH
of a
DOVE

GRISELDA GIFFORD

TWO FALCONS PRESS

Published by Two Falcons Press
10 Dukes Ride, Leighton Buzzard LU7 3JS
Tel & Fax: 01525 374479
e-mail: Griseldagifford@aol.com
www.Griselda.co.uk

ISBN 978-0-9955883-2-5

ACKNOWLEDGEMENT

*My thanks to Dick Richardson of Country Books for his help
and also to fellow authors, Margaret Nash and Stephanie Baudet,
for their encouragement.*

Printed and bound in England by:
4edge Ltd. Hockley, Essex

DEDICATION

To Jim

And in memory of my mother, nicknamed Taddy –
who won swimming races in the river Ouse.

CHAPTER 1

I stopped eating my tea, sensing the battle to come. Our country was at war with Germany but this explosion was in our home, a fight between my elder brother, Alex, and my father.

Alex was standing in the doorway, talking fast. "Father – they're recruiting in the town. I saw them on the way back from school. I'm going to join the Army just as soon as I can."

For once I was glad my father was blind because my brother's blue eyes were angry and defiant. Mother's hand, holding the teapot, shook and the teacup she was filling overflowed onto the cloth. My little brother, Jimmy, stopped chewing with his mouth full and his eyes opened wide. He worshipped Alex and thought anything he said was wonderful.

Father sat quite still, his mouth tight. His square-cut beard always made him look severe but now I knew he was really angry.

I knew there would be an explosion so I plunged in recklessly, "I saw them – the recruiting officers – there was a stupid notice saying something about your girlfriend would be ashamed of you if you didn't join up. I hate this stupid war!"

"Beatrice and Jimmy, please leave the table," Father said. "This isn't anything to do with you."

I was annoyed being treated like a child when I was nearly sixteen now and about to start work but I knew better than to argue.

"It's not fair," Jimmy said when we left the kitchen. "Why should Alex be in trouble if he wants to join up as soon as he's seventeen?"

"He's only just sixteen now, too young to enlist, and Father is against this war. He thinks Christians shouldn't kill. And we have some German blood – remember those Christmas cards from Cousin Frederick?"

Jimmy was pulling at a clump of his curly fair hair and sucking his thumb, so I knew he was upset because his hero, Alex, had been told off.

"So why are we fighting Germans?"

I didn't know how to answer. I wasn't exactly sure why this war with Germany had started, in 1914, over a year ago now, but already two young men from the village had been killed and life was changing and uncertain.

Jimmy went outside our cottage and marched up and down with a stick over his shoulder. "I'm going to be a soldier, whatever you say, Taddy."

Alex began calling me Tadpole, after I won swimming competitions in the river Ouse and somehow it had stuck, despite our parents' disapproval.

Tommy, the pony who pulled our 'governess' cart, came trotting up to the back door for an apple. I leaned against his warm flank for comfort; I was totally sick of Alex and the way he stirred up Father and teased me. After all, he was still at the grammar school because he was supposed to be so clever and I'd offered to leave school to earn money to help our family. In a way, I would be paying for Alex to stay on at school but he wasn't likely to thank me for it.

But I had my own secret ambition – I wanted to be an actress. I hoped that going to work as a nursemaid for the Rossiters, who were rumoured to entertain artistic folk of all sorts, would be my first step.

I walked past the small ivy-clad privy, where I sometimes

escaped to be on my own, ignoring the strong smell of tar. Our cottage is on a hill and I looked down our small field to the water-meadows which led to the river Ouse. Beyond the river, I could see the setting sun outlining the barley-sugar twists of the chimneys of Tanglemere, the Rossiters' house. Three wild swans flew over the sun-gilded water, winging their way home for the night.

Tommy wandered towards his stable, next to the tumble-down shed which Alex called his workshop. He'd told me if I went inside he'd throw all my books into the river. I didn't doubt his word because he'd buried my dolls when I was younger, so they were mouldy when I found them. I thought crossly of the day when I had been sitting peacefully on Tommy's warm back, and Alex smacked the pony's rump so he trotted under the washing-line. I was hooked off by my chin! I'd tried to hit Alex then but he'd just run away, laughing.

Jimmy ran down the hill to the river. "Don't get wet!" I called after him.

Then I walked towards the shed. I was too old to be scared of my brother and his stupid secrets. I was lifting the latch to the door when I heard a sound behind me. Everything went black as I struggled against smelly sacking. "I told you never go in my shed. It's private!" Alex shouted.

I fought hard, kicking out with my tough leather boots and I heard Alex shout as I hit his shin.

"Nasty slimy Tadpole!" Alex shouted but I threw off the sack and saw my brother hopping on one leg. Tommy came up to me, ears forward, probably wondering what was happening.

Tucking my skirt into my bloomers I jumped on the pony, kicking his sides so he trotted down the slope and through the reedy marsh to the river. Suddenly he put his head down to eat the long grass and I slid down his neck, landing with a thump.

I looked back, hoping Alex hadn't seen me fall off but he'd

3

disappeared into his shed. According to him, he was inventing something brilliant but he was always boasting so I didn't take any notice.

I patted Tommy, to show I didn't bear him any ill will, undid my boots and pushed through the branches to my special old willow-tree, pulling myself up to the branch that overhung the river.

This was another place where I could escape on my own, where I brought books to read, practised my songs and acted little bits of Shakespeare's plays where nobody could laugh at me.

Even my best friend, Jem Mason, had never been here. It was totally my place, where I could let the real Beatrice out, no longer Mother's quiet, helpful Bea, nor Alex's teased Taddy – but Beatrice the Beautiful and Brilliant.

I thought of Mrs. Rossiter, my new employer, who had dazzled all the family except Father, when she came to see if I would be allowed to work for her. Mother had heard – through the village gossip – that the 'new folk' who had bought Tanglemere, needed a Governess to replace a young women who had gone to train as an ambulance driver in London, helping people who had been wounded in Zeppelin attacks. I had written to Mrs. Rossiter, enclosing a reference from the my High School Head Mistress.

Then she had suddenly appeared, just as our cat, Floss, had brought in a dead mouse and Jimmy ran in, covered in mud. I'd never seen anyone with the new bobbed hair before, nor a lady visiting without wearing a hat and wearing a bright blue silky dress which only came to mid-calf. I was glad Father couldn't see the rouge delicately applied to her cheeks and lips but he must have smelled the glorious musky flower scent she wore and heard her beautiful voice.

I wanted to tell Jimmy not to stare at her. I suppose he'd never seen anyone dressed like that.

I looked round now. Jimmy – where was he? I'd told him

not to play too close to the river, which flowed swift and strong just here. Perhaps he'd gone back to the house.

I peered through the willow-leaves. Further down the bank the filtered sunlight caught Jimmy's blonde hair. He was just along the bank, thrusting his arm deep into the water. He must be imitating Jem's brother and my childhood friend, Tod, who caught trout by moving his fingers gently under the fish and then bringing the poor creature out.

I heard a faint cry and big splash as Jimmy overbalanced and fell in.

I scrambled down the tree, tearing my skirt. I stepped out of it and jumped into the river, swimming as fast as I could, hampered by my petticoat and bloomers, to where Jimmy was flailing the water. He clung on to me and dragged us both down to the muddy depths. The water was still spring-cold and gave me a slight shock. I am sure I would have managed to save him myself but someone else was in the water, pulling us both out, one after the other and dumping us on the bank.

"Are you all right?" asked a voice..

I stared up at him. He was probably Alex's age, tall and thin and naked to the waist, wearing only long and soaking woollen underpants. I blushed and looked away from the sight.

I turned on Jimmy who was coughing up water. "You stupid boy! You can hardly swim and I told you not to go too near the river."

The boy smiled and his whole face lit up. "I'm just back from boarding-school and I couldn't resist a swim – just stripped off my clothes. Lucky I saw you."

"I could have saved him myself. I have learned life-saving," I said, getting up and wishing my petticoat wasn't clinging to me quite so much.

Then I thought I wasn't being very polite. "Thank you anyway," I added.

"Life saving – unusual for a girl." He looked at me as if I

were some strange specimen in a Zoo.

"Why?" I spoke crossly, ashamed of being seen in my underclothes. "It's 1915 now, you know, not the olden days. Women are driving buses and trams and I've heard they may be able to vote later on."

He stared at me, then grinned, showing perfect white teeth. I suppose I was chattering on to cover my embarrassment and now he would think I was an idiot.

"Taddy's won swimming races in the river," Jimmy said. He presumably thought he'd be in less trouble if he buttered me up.

"Has she? Perhaps, Taddy, we can have a race one day?" He was still smiling, laughing at me. Drops of water were running off his muscular arms. I looked away again, quickly.

"And she sings too," Jimmy added. "She's in a concert tomorrow at the church hall."

"Jimmy! That's enough! We have to go," I snapped

The boy had the nerve to stand in the way, and grasped my hand in his. "My name is Oberon. Well met, proud Titania!"

How could anybody be called Oberon? He was teasing me, just as Alex did.

I snatched my hand away. "You might as well know the quote is "well met by moonlight, proud Titania." Come, Jimmy, we must go home."

Then I remembered I had to fetch my boots and skirt so we went along the bank. Something perverse inside me longed to look back but I heard a low laugh and then a splash, as he dived into the river.

"You weren't very nice to him, Taddy," Jimmy complained as I put my skirt over my wet petticoat and thrust my damp feet into my boots.

"He was kind to help but he's a perfect stranger. You had better not tell Father about him."

"Then you won't tell how I fell in?" Jimmy asked cunningly, looking up at me with his deceptively innocent blue eyes.

"I'll see," I said.

Of course I got into trouble with Father for letting Jimmy fall in. It wasn't fair – I'd rescued my silly little brother but I didn't tell tales about his guddling for trout. Mother was more concerned about my getting so wet. "You don't want to catch cold for the Concert tomorrow, Bea. I am just hoping your father won't disapprove of what we have made for you to wear."

I gave her a damp hug. She'd been such an angel, secretly altering my outfit from clothes I'd found in our dressing-up chest in the attic and I had practised alone in my room.

"We used to do little plays at home," she'd said. "I had dreams of being an actress myself but…" She didn't have to finish. I had never met our grandparents but knew them to be so wealthy and snobbish that they cut her off completely when she ran away with Father. I suppose a poor and blind music teacher wasn't the match they'd hoped for. I hated them for that. Father might have a country accent and no money to offer, but he was a million times more gifted than the stuck-up landowners they'd have preferred.

"I used to love hearing you sing in the church choir," she said. "So I know you'll be a great success with your secret act, whatever it is. No need to be nervous tomorrow."

I put a confident smile on my face. "You have no need to worry," I said but a million butterflies were churning in my stomach as I spoke.

CHAPTER 2

I felt sick. "Are you all right, Bea?" my friend Jem Mason asked.

"Yes," I said faintly. Here we were, back-stage in the stuffy Church Hall. I could hear the hum of voices beyond the threadbare curtains. All the proceeds from the concert were for comforts for the soldiers out in France and nearly everyone in the village would be there.

Jem hated singing or reciting so she was bossing the little ones and helping with the curtains and arranging the backdrop – a huge Union Jack and a vase of red, white and blue flowers.

Now she was peeping through a gap in the curtains. "The Drummonds have brought some of their wounded officers to watch! And Elizabeth Drummond's brother Edwin is there – golly, he's not bad-looking in that officer's uniform."

Elizabeth Drummond came up to us. Ready for her piano solo, she was wearing a white poplin dress, embroidered with flowers. I noticed she'd already put her hair up and adorned it with a white rose.

"I'm really proud of Edwin," she said. "He led his troops in a big battle and he's been promoted already."

Once, we'd all been great friends, Elizabeth, Jem, and her brother Tod and me – and occasionally Edwin, although he was older and went fishing and shooting with Tod. We used to play hide-and-seek all round the .many rooms at the Manor or had hay fights at the Masons' farm – but Elizabeth had

8

recently been away at some snooty girls school and she'd suddenly become a Young Lady. I'd met her, riding side-saddle, instead of cantering bare-back through the woods and she gave me a gracious wave, just as if she were Royalty, instead of inviting me back to the house.

Fortunately, I don't think she heard Jem mutter, "They made Edwin an officer because he was a toff and went to a public school." Jem could be very tactless at times.

Elizabeth was too busy staring at me. "Bea! What on earth are you wearing!" she shrieked.

"Just my outfit for my song," I snapped.

I twirled my silver-tipped stick so she jumped back. Even Jem had stared at my smart black jacket and trousers. I'd stuffed my wild red hair into the old black top-hat that we'd found in the attic and I was wearing Mother's white kid gloves. I'd used a piece of coal to black in a moustache.

"Fancy dressing as a man!" Elizabeth said scornfully.

Then we had to be quiet, as the Vicar was booming at the audience about the concert for Our Brave Troops who were fightingr the Evil Hun.

I wondered if the Germans were praying for their Brave Troops fighting the Evil English.

Jem ordered us to go back-stage except for Elizabeth, who would play the piano.

As I passed her, standing by the piano, she whispered, "Oh – I wish I hadn't said I would like to be first." She sounded nervous and suddenly I liked her better.

"Father says you're one of his best pupils," I whispered back.

She did play well, I had to admit. Now it was my turn to be nervous as our Jimmy followed with a solo in his pure choir-boy voice, "*O for the Wings of a Dove*"

I had to wait for Miss Hebbes, from the Post Office, to sing "*Come into the Garden, Maude*," with Father accompanying her and followed by the Vicar's wife singing "*Keep the Home*

Fires Burning," in a quavery soprano.

Then – my turn. "We now have Beatrice Denning with a mystery song," the Vicar boomed. "She will sing unaccompanied."

I hadn't dared ask Father to accompany me on the piano – I knew he would disapprove because he was so old-fashioned.

My stomach did a somersault but I squared my shoulders and marched on to the stage, twirling my stick. The trousers made me feel free as I strode along and I really felt I was a man!

I bowed to the audience. There was a hush but somebody giggled.

"*I am Burlington Bertie from Bow!*" I said, then sang, as I marched up and down

People began to laugh and someone clapped when I came to the second verse,

"*I'm Burlington Bertie, I rise at ten-thirty*
And saunter along like a toff..."

When I came to the bit when Bertie says "*Toodle Oo*" to the Queen, someone shouted, "Shame!"

It sounded like old Major Trottman, one of the Churchwardens, and I suppose he thought it was disrespectful to the Queen. There was a silence, and I felt a creeping disappointment but suddenly everyone clapped and shouts of "Encore!" came from the front row of wounded officers.

Who was that at the back of the hall, standing with Alex, Tod, and other young men from the village? Tall with thick dark hair and now – a big smile directly at me as he went on clapping longer than the others.

I could feel my face burning as I bowed and marched off the stage.

"You're dark horse, Bea Denning!" Jem said. "That gave them something to clap about! What will your Da say? He's so strict, isn't he? Mind you, at least your parents came along. Mine were too busy at the farm, as usual, but at least my brother came along. Who was that boy standing next to our Tod? The one that was clapping so hard?"

I suddenly realised where I'd seen him before – in the river. "I have no idea," I lied. I was still flustered and thinking he had seen me in my soaking underwear. Then I had a wicked wish for one moment, that my wet blouse had clung to a more curvaceous figure than mine.

The concert ended with all of us on stage leading the singing of *Land and Hope and Glory* and *Rule Britannia!* And of course, *God Save the King.*

Elizabeth came up to me when we left the hall and I was waiting for our parents… "Your song went quite well," she said in a patronising voice. "Of course, it wasn't quite right for the church hall."

Her brother Edwin came over. "Oh, come on Lizzie. She was splendid. All the chaps loved the song." He smiled at me but his parents gave a small wave and walked on to their carriage. I guessed they didn't approve.

I had pushed the River Boy – as I called him – to the back of my mind and I was worrying what Father was going to say to me. At least he couldn't see my costume but no doubt someone would remark on it and the song was from the Music Hall, not at all approved by Father, I am sure.

Of course, Alex was a tell-tale as usual. As we walked home, he said to Father,

"I wish you could have seen Bea – dressed up as a man. It suited her, except bits of her hair kept coming down. Fancy my little sister singing a music hall song!"

I tried to kick his ankle with my tough button-boot but missed.

"I told you, David, Beatrice looked perfectly splendid," Mother said quickly. "We made the costume together." I knew she said this because Father loved her so much he almost never got cross with *her*.

Jimmy winked at me. "I think Bea was terrific." He began

11

to march along beside us, singing what he could remember of my song, stumbling in the semi-darkness. The village had taken fright after hearing of Zeppelin bombings, and all curtains were closed so light couldn't guide the huge airships our way.

Father was quiet then, walking carefully on the cobbles, guided by Mother, although he always joked he was better in the dark then anyone because he was used to it. But when we got back to the cottage, clustering in the kitchen while Mother made cocoa all round, he put his hand on my shoulder and delivered a short lecture:

"You have a lovely and true voice, Beatrice. I had hoped you would practise with me and we would choose a traditional song."

"I wanted to surprise everyone." My voice was low because I didn't like to disappoint my father even though I was beginning to fight against his strict, old-fashioned ideas just as I fought against wearing a corset. I wanted freedom...

"I gather the Rossiters have connections with artists and the stage," he went on. "And the parents are living apart at the moment. I want you to be very careful not to be influenced by a modern, fast set, Beatrice. Their morals may not be the same as ours."

I thought about this on Sunday, as I pumped the organ for him. If I stopped, the music would stop, so I couldn't let my thoughts wander too much but I had noticed Edwin was missing from the Drummonds' pew. Had he gone back to France? And there were two nurses with four soldiers from the Drummonds' hospital wing. I told myself not to grumble about having to pump the organ, at least I had both arms, un- like one of the men. There was another soldier, with a bandaged head and an eye patch and two men on crutches. Outside, the sun shone on our peaceful village but now the war was coming closer, and I hated it.

After lunch, Mother asked me to fetch milk from the farm.

I wanted to talk to Jem but I was scared of cows, ever since I had been chased by a herd of bullocks, when I was quite young. I walked along the lane towards Berry Farm, deciding whether I dared cross the cow-field, which was quicker, or go round by road.

The warm sun brought out the heavy scent from the May blossom on the hedges and I longed to swim but it was against Father's rules for Sunday. I was supposed to read, sew or practise the piano but it wasn't fair, because Alex was already out on his bicycle and I knew Jimmy would play with his friends after Sunday School.

Suddenly there was the sound of a motor-car engine and a big open car zoomed past me. Someone was honking the horn and Mrs. Rossiter was waving her hand at me as she drove by, a filmy scarf fluttering from her neck. The car left a cloud of dust which covered my white Sunday blouse.

That would be something to tell Jem.

Now I was by the stile and I could see the roof of Berry Farm in the distance.

Not a cow in sight. Perhaps they were already in the barn, being milked. I told myself I wasn't going to get far with my secret career if I couldn't even face a few cows.

I got over the stile and walked swiftly down the field. Then I heard a loud mooing and the whole herd was walking out of the little wood at the edge of the field, straight across my path. I couldn't move.

Then I thought of all those soldiers having to advance under fire, bullets flying everywhere. How could I be a coward and run from harmless cows? I began to sing 'Burlington Bertie' and marched on like a soldier. The nearest cows stared, amazed, mooed, then trotted off. My heart thudded and I didn't look behind me as I went on, singing and marching but I thought I heard a mooing and a swishing of tails.

Jem's brother Tod was opening the gate into the farmyard and laughing at me. "You've got a new audience, Bea! Thank you for bringing the cows in for milking."

I looked behind me. The cows were following me, keeping a few yards behind, their ears forward as they listened.

"I liked the song in the hall but it sounds even better outside," Tod said. "But I like you in a dress best of all, Bea."

I'd known him all my life but suddenly I felt a little shy. He seemed taller and older and he was looking at me in a strange way.

We stood together as the cows plodded past, full udders swinging. I could smell his skin and hair, a slightly musky, man-smell overlaid by a Sunday wash with Lifebuoy soap and I noticed a cut on his chin. He'd been shaving – suddenly he'd turned into a young man.

Bars of sunlight filtered through the high windows of the milking shed, striping the cows as they came in. "Come to help?" Jem asked. She was helping her father tether each cow in its stall. I could smell their milky breath as they passed but I didn't move an inch.

Jem was almost as tall and broad-shouldered as her brother and she'd screwed her hair into a flat cap so she looked like a strong lad instead of a girl of fifteen like me.

"I've come for milk." I waved the jug at her.

"I saw you marching past the cows. They didn't like your song, did they?" She laughed. "Ma's in the Dairy. Has your dad got over your music hall act?"

"Not quite."

"Well, you'll be acting the young lady tomorrow at the Rossiters, won't you." She laughed.

"I've just seen her, driving a wonderful new car."

"What make was it?" Tod had closed the gate and walked up to us.

"Alex says it's a De Dion Bouton."

He whistled. "They must be rich! Bea – I thought your song was wonderful." He added in a gentle, affectionate voice. "Leave the can with our mam. I just want to show you our latest arrival."

He put his hand on my arm to steer me clear of the smelly heap of cow-dug piled at the side of the yard. Tod – who only last Christmas pushed Jem and me into a pile of turkey feathers so we sneezed our heads off and feathers fluttered like leaves up into the high barn roof. Now he was treating me like a young lady.

At the back of the yard, there was a fenced off grassy enclosure with a shed at one end. Tod called softy and a beautiful black mare came out and trotted up to us.

She had one white fetlock and a white star on her face. Now I'd often dreamed when sitting on our sturdy Tommy – of riding out on a beautiful horse and here was the horse of my dreams.

"She's mine – my grandad left me some money," Tod said. "We're going to breed from her – we know someone with a thoroughbred stallion.." He stopped and I saw he was blushing, perhaps thinking I knew little of the facts of life but Jem and the farm had educated me.

He unlatched the gate to the yard. "Star's high-spirited but gentle. Come and talk to her."

The mare was wearing a halter and he held her while I stroked her smooth neck.

"Could I just sit on her back? Would she mind?" I asked.

"In that dress?"

I tucked my bulky skirt into my bloomers. Red-faced at the sight, Tod gave me a leg-up. Then he walked the mare round.

I loved the shiny warmth of her between my legs and I felt like a Queen on her back. I spoke to her as she walked. "Come on, Star," I whispered and in a moment she had sprung into a gentle trot. Tod shouted something as the halter-rope spun out of his hand but I wasn't scared. She broke into a canter now, going straight at the fence. I clung on to her mane as I felt her hindquarters gathering under me to jump.

I leaned forward and called her name in a mixture of fear

15

and joy as she cleared the fence. I slid forward and almost fell as she landed, then recovered my balance and I felt truly alive as she cantered across the next field. I could hear Tod calling and the larks shrilling above and I looked at her ears, pricked forward and knew Star was happy too.

Then she swerved to the trees at the side of the field.

I tried to duck under a branch but I was too late and I was swept off her back, landing in something soft and squidgy.

CHAPTER 3

I struggled up from the cow-pat, smelly and aching and looked round for Star. Alex would be so upset if she were lost. Supposing she strayed onto the road? There were very few motor-cars in our area but I imagined Mrs. Rossiter driving along at speed, rounding a bend and then meeting Star, galloping loose down the road.

I hobbled on, calling the mare and feeling ridiculous. How could I fall off two horses in as many days? Our pony knew his name and would come to us but Tod's mare had only just arrived.

"Bea! Bea!" Tod's voice. I looked back and saw him far off, running towards me. I had to find Star before he caught up with me.

I was in a wheat-field at the edge of a little wood, under the low branches that had swept me off the mare's back. I could see right down into the valley to the silver thread of the river and I could not see the mare. Then I heard a whinnying from the wood and saw hoof marks going down a narrow track between the trees.

I ran down the track, still calling and then I saw her, plunging and pulling at the halter which was somehow caught in a thick bush. "Star!" I walked forward slowly, talking to her all the time in a low voice.

She stopped moving and stared at me, her ears pricked.

Slowly, slowly I went up to her, my hand outstretched, still talking and I caught hold of her halter. Her head reared up but

I hung on to her with one hand, with the other, trying to un-tangle the rope.

"Bea!" Tod was there. "I'll hold her while you deal with the rope," he said. "Are you all right? I saw you from the field gate but I didn't see you fall."

"It was a branch, swept me off." I tugged at the rope, my hands scratched from the prickly holly bush and at last freed it. "I'm sorry – I couldn't stop her. Don't get too near – I fell in a cow-pat."

If I hadn't known him since we were little children, I'd have been more embarrassed because my white Sunday blouse was smeared with cow-manure and I must be stinking to high heaven.

He held Star firmly but turned to me, smiling. "I don't mind about the muck on you, Bea – I can't keep away from you and that's the truth." Suddenly he put his free arm round me, drawing me close to him and so close to Star that his male scent mingled with the comforting horse-smell I'd always liked. "Will you wait for me – so we can be wed one day? You're so lovely, Bea."

Before I could move, he kissed me very gently on the lips. I had never before been kissed by a boy and I have to admit I liked it, although I drew back, surprised.

"Can't we just stay friends? I'm much too young to promise anything." How could I explain about my secret ambition? I was very fond of Tod and often wished he were my brother instead of Alex – but I didn't want to be tied by marriage and children.

He began to lead Star back along the path. "Better hurry back and clean you up. Your mother's waiting for the milk and it is Sunday, after all. I should never have put you on the mare. It was my fault. Sorry. And I shouldn't have kissed you."

He didn't look at me as he strode back.

I'd hurt his feelings but what could I do? "It was nice," I

said feebly.

Nice? More than nice but I imagined how horrified and angry Father would be if he knew what had happened.

Jem was vaulting over the gate in her usual unladylike way as we came back. "Tod!" she called. "What have you done to Bea? I heard you calling her and then found Star had got out."

I didn't want Tod to get into trouble so I said, quickly, "I wanted to ride her round the paddock but something scared her and she jumped out. Then I was swept off by a branch"

"You should have seen the mare jump, Jem," Tod said. "That fence must be five foot at least."

Jem clapped him on the back, more a smack than in a friendly way. "Bea's only used to riding that old pony. Whatever got into you? She'll be in big trouble when she gets back. And it's a good thing that Da is up Longacre checking the sheep or he'd be after you."

She was two years younger than Tod but sometimes she seemed older and tended to boss him about a bit too much. Maybe it was because she was so tall and strong and her father treated her like a boy, expecting her to do all kinds of farm work. She was even wearing an old pair of Tod's breeches, and on a Sunday, too.

"You'd better get that mud off," she said after Tod had put Star back in her paddock. "And I've got to get back to the milking."

I washed off some of the mud in the stone sink and Jem loaned me a patched old pinafore, which was so big on me that it came almost to my ankles.

She wished me luck with my new post with the Rossiters. "I've heard she's pretty free and easy with her children. Modern ways, they say." Jem smiled. "But you'll cope, Bea, I'm sure. Come round and tell me how it goes."

"Will you be all right, Bea?" Tod asked. "I'd come with you only I have work to do, even on a Sunday." Suddenly he grasped my hand. "I'm happy just to be friends, at the moment," he said. His fingers were rough but warm and comforting.

I felt relieved and yet – a bit sorry but I smiled as I said goodbye.

As I walked down our lane, making up excuses as to why I was so long – I heard a horse's hooves and the creaking of harness and the Drummonds' smart trap came past, drawn by a shining bay horse. Elizabeth sat very upright, the reins in her hands and her mother beside her. To my horror, she slowed the horse down to a walk and lent over, her large hat at an angle. "What have you been up to, Beatrice? Rolling in the mud?"

"Good afternoon, Beatrice," Lady Drummond said with a disapproving nod that made the black feathers on her hat quiver. "We are going to see your future employer, Mrs. Rossiter, who will begin work at the Manor Hospital tomorrow. Such a blessing, as she has nursing experience. I believe you are to be the new nursery-maid."

It was hard to look dignified when I was so dirty but I said, "I am to be the girls' governess."

"Ah, a governess." Lady Drummond's tone was sarcastic.

Elizabeth was hiding a smile behind her white kid glove. "Will your duties allow you to come to my birthday picnic next week? I will be sending out invitations. And please bring your brother. It's a special occasion, becoming sixteen. I could get married." And she preened herself in her usual conceited way. I pitied anyone who married her.

"Alexander will miss our Edwin," her mother said sadly and, although I thought her stuck-up and snobbish I was sorry for her then.

They drove on, Elizabeth waving at me, still smirking at the thought of little Bea becoming a governess? Well, it wasn't likely that Alex would come to the party – he liked Edwin but avoided Elizabeth, who had a crush on him. He said she was far too young for him.

I tried to creep in by the back gate. Although I'd washed my face and hands I could still smell the cow-dung on me and there was a great scratch down my face from the tree branch.

Of course, Alex would come out of his shed just as I went through the back door. "Taddy, what are you wearing? And you stink of cows!" He laughed.

I didn't deign to reply but of course Jimmy came running out of the back door, his face shining clean for once and wearing his best clothes. I knew how late it was then, because he was dressed for Sunday School. "You've been ages and ages. Did you have to milk the cow yourself?" he asked, giggling as he ran out of the gate.

I had hoped Mother was resting on the old horsehair sofa in the front room, listening to Father's usual Sunday relaxation between services, playing Bach on the piano but she must have heard me put the big can of milk on the kitchen table.

She looked me up and down with a serious face instead of her usual smile. "You have been over an hour, Bea, and the farm is only ten minutes walk away. And why are you wearing that huge pinny? And there's a smell..."

Again, I didn't want to get Tod into trouble so I said, "Oh, I fell over in a cow-pat. Jem lent me the pinny."

She looked at me sharply. I stared at my dirty boots, to avoid her penetrating blue stare. I didn't like lying to her – and now I had another secret, Tod's kiss.

Mother sighed. "I was going to pump the organ myself tonight, to give you a rest but I think in the circumstances you should help Father."

"It's not fair, you never ask Alex," I muttered.

"Last time he stopped pumping twice. I found he was doing a drawing of one of his inventions at the same time. You will have to grow up a good deal if you are going to set an example to Mrs. Rossiters' girls. Now, change and tidy yourself up. After all, it is Sunday."

How could I forget? Mr. Fairweather, the Vicar, was old and

kept repeating the same sermon and I didn't like being hidden away in the organ loft. Sometimes I longed to stand up in the church and sing, "*Daisy, Daisy, give me your answer do,*" or even, for those poor wounded soldiers, "*Pack up your troubles in your old kit bag and* SMILE SMILE SMILE!"

If I were God, I'd be so bored by our gloomy services that I'd just go to sleep.

One of our Grandfather clocks struck the hour, followed at one minute intervals by the others. Father's clever hands had never got them to strike together, reminding me of time passing and that I had to start work tomorrow. My stomach churned. Then I told myself not to be silly, the girls were only eight and ten years old.

Mrs. Rossiter had mentioned a much older brother who was at an Art School in London but I supposed he would live away from home.

As I washed in the big stone sink, I imagined myself teaching them to sing and act. Mrs. Rossiter would come to watch them take part in little plays with me, and she would tell her artistic London friends how gifted I was – and then...

Someone was rattling the bolted scullery door. "Hurry up! I suppose it's you, Taddy," Alex said loudly. I'm covered in oil from mending my cycle and I'm to join Eddie, shooting rabbits at the Manor."

"On a Sunday. Father won't like it."

"He won't know unless you sneak on me. Eddie's going back tomorrow, to his regiment, lucky blighter. I hope the war lasts long enough for me to join up."

I felt the usual surge of annoyance with my brother. "That's so selfish – so like you, Alex! Think of all the people being killed. But I wish you could join the Army and give me a bit of peace here."

"Poor little Taddy! Does your nasty big bro. tease you too much, then?"

I didn't answer but I took even longer to finish washing.

That night, I was awake a long time, planning lessons and outings for the girls. I vowed to be a good governess to them, then Mrs. Rossiter would be so pleased she would introduce me into the glittering world of the Arts, and particularly the Theatre.

CHAPTER 4

I was so nervous the next morning that I couldn't eat my breakfast.

Mother gave me a hug. "Just be firm but loving, Bea dear," she advised.

I wanted to arrive at Tanglemere looking like a young lady, so I didn't tuck my skirt up and it kept getting mixed up with the wheel because the cycle was old and had no skirt guard.

It was another hot day and I could feel sweat creeping down the back of my high-necked white blouse as I cycled through the open gates and up the drive.

The last owner of Tanglemere had been a reclusive old man who threatened visitors with a shot-gun, so I'd never seen the house close to. The sun shone on mellow bricks and glinted on diamond-paned windows but part of the front was smothered in thick ivy, making the house look mysterious. I imagined some imprisoned mad women in one of the attic rooms, like Mr. Rochester's crazy wife in *Jane Eyre*. Mother had caught me with her copy of the book and told me not to tell Father, who would think it far too old and daring for me to read.

The effect was rather spoiled by the latest de Dion Bouton car outside the house.

I thought I saw a face at the window, then the front door opened and two great dogs came leaping out, barking and growling, followed by the girls, barefoot and clad only in faded blue cotton shifts that showed their skinny sunburnt legs. "Mind they don't eat you!" shouted the elder girl, who must be Persephone. At least I knew their names from my interview but I rather wished I had met the girls first.

The younger girl, Hermione, stared at me, chewing a lock of her untidy long hair..

Although my heart was beating fast, I was determined not to show nervousness so I put my hand out to the leading dog, a great hairy creature. Jem – used to farm dogs – would have been totally calm so I pretended I was Jem – I drew myself up to my five foot two inches and talked to the dog, "Good boy. Come here."

He stopped growling and waved his long tail as I stroked the wiry hair on his head. The other dog came up on my other side – enclosed by the big dogs I smiled at the girls, determined to be friendly, but firm. "You must be Persephone and your little sister is Hermione," I said wondering how a mother as fashion-conscious as Mrs. Rossiter could let them go out like workhouse children – and they at least had boots to wear.

The girl scowled at me. "We hate our names. I'm Perse and she's Hermie. I told Seli we didn't need a nursemaid now we're so old," she said.

I wondered who Seli was. "I am going to be your governess, not a nursemaid." I tried hard to sound older.

"We had one of those but she left." Perse giggled. "She didn't like it when I locked her in the nursery."

"She smelled of mothballs and wore fusty dusty clothes. Fusty, dusty!" Herme chanted, dancing up and down.

Should I tell them off for being rude? But I wanted them to like me. Could I manage these strange, rowdy girls?

"I suppose you had better come in," Perse muttered ungraciously.

The dogs followed us into a dark, oak-panelled hall.

"She's here, Seli!" Perse yelled.

"Please don't shout, Persephone." Mrs. Rossiter was hurrying down the staircase, dressed in a nurse's uniform. Her bobbed hair was drawn under a tall white hat and she still looked beautiful, even in those severe clothes.

The dogs ran to her. "So the dogs welcomed you, Beatrice?" She smiled at me.

"She looked scared," Perse said.

"I was not," I lied. Did she expect me to call her Seli? I couldn't believe the children were allowed to use her first name.

"The bigger one is Tara, my Irish Wolfhound, and the other is Dante, our Retriever. Now, Beatrice, I am just off to the Manor Hospital. I trained as a nurse before the War and I am glad to go back, even though..." She stopped a moment. "Even though I'm used to illness, the sight of so much suffering makes me very sad."

"Shall I begin with a lesson?" I asked. I had brought a simple reading book and exercises I'd once done myself at their age.

I thought the sound came from the dogs but realised the girls were groaning quietly. Mrs. Rossiter frowned at them. "Girls! You have to listen to Miss Denning." Then she put her hand on my arm. "They need structure to their day but I do not believe in punishment. Breakfast first, I think. Mrs. Maggs is in the kitchen I shall hear how the day went when I get back."

Then she was gone and I heard the car start up with a great roar.

"What about shoes, first?" I said.

"We only wear shoes outside the grounds," Herme said. "Seli believes our feet need to breathe."

I felt as if I were in a kind of Alice in Wonderland world, so different from my own and the feeling grew worse when the girls ate bowls of nuts and fruit, grudgingly cut up by Mrs. Maggs, the cook, who had to stop kneading bread dough. There was no sign of toast or porridge.

"Keep those demons out of my way," Mrs. Maggs slapped Perse's hand as she grabbed a bit of dough. "I can tell you,

Miss Denning, these girls need a firm hand. Now the maids have left, I'm right on the edge of giving in my notice." Her big red face glowered as she scowled at the girls clapping and giggling.

I hurried them out into the garden. "We could look for leaves and flowers to study."

I had to run to keep up with them as they danced round the large neglected garden where rabbits ran through the tall grasses and roses tumbled down from broken arbours

Herme suddenly put her hand in mine and I felt happier. "Would you like to see the maze, Miss Denning?"

I was sweating even more in the heat and path between the tall yew hedges looked cool and shady. The girls ran ahead, laughing.

"Wait for me!" I called and then I thought that sounded undignified. They thought I would get lost but I would show them I could find my way.

I took one turning, then the next. Enclosed by the strong-smelling yew hedges it was stiflingly hot and I became angry. "Come out at once or I shall punish you!" I called but I only heard the echo of a laugh.

Why had I taken on these wild, out-of-hand children? I was close to angry tears when I saw a brightness ahead and I was out of the maze.

I wouldn't wait for the girls. I would go back to the house, have a drink of water and cycle home. There must be some other work I could do. Father was right – this family was too unconventional. I would not look after little savages but resign and look for another position.

The maze was at the end of the big garden and I hurried down an overgrown path towards a brick wall. I thought it was part of the house but when I grew near, I saw I'd turned the wrong way. This was an outbuilding or barn. The two dogs lay outside in the sun, seeming to guard an open door.

Music wafted out, music I knew – a song from the Mikado,

by the famous Gilbert and Sullivan. Mother says one of my besetting sins is curiosity and I had to know who was in the barn.

Dante and Tara got to their feet as I approached but I spoke to them and, my heart beating fast, I peered inside. Immediately I was hit by a wave of colour – paintings were stacked round the white-washed walls. I could see the back of an easel. I had to know who was painting.

The music was going at full blast from a big gramophone gleaming in the corner and the artist never heard me approach.

He turned round and saw me.

"Ah – my Titania! We meet again." He smiled hugely and waved a paint daubed brush. He wore a smock covered with paint and a blue splodge was on his nose.

It was the cheeky young man who had rescued me from the river.

Oberon.

Chapter 5

"Oh – it's you!" was all I could say.

He smiled again. "It's certainly me! And you aren't just a water-sprite but Miss Denning, fierce governess for my terrible sisters. So you have a double life. Music hall artiste and teacher."

He was laughing at me and although this made me cross, I couldn't help noticing his dark-lashed brown eyes were flecked with amber and the way his curly black hair framed his fine features. He had a look of the young Byron, the poet, I thought.

His voice was low and pleasing as he said, "After seeing you perform, I told Selina – my mother – that you would be able to teach my sisters acting and singing – if they would listen. Ever since my father went to live in London, they have misbehaved. I think they miss him. Come and see my painting."

I moved forward but he put a paint-daubed hand on my shoulder. "Stand back a little," he said. "It shows better that way."

Now I noticed he'd set up a still life arrangement of fruit and orange marigolds in a blue vase, against a filmy blue scarf, shot with orange.

Oberon's painting sang with colour, applied in many small splodges which somehow mixed together to dazzle the eye.

"It's in the Impressionist style," he said.

I had vaguely heard of the Impressionists but I had never

visited an art gallery.

He was standing so near me I could smell the oil paint smeared on his smock – and yet I didn't really want him to move away.

"I like it," I said. "It makes me feel happy. Did you know you have paint on your nose?"

He fetched an oily rag and wiped his face, his dark eyebrows raised comically. "I'm as bad as my father – he gets in a real mess when he's right into a portrait." He hesitated, then said, "Would you sit for me? I would like to paint your portrait. You have such wonderful red hair against your creamy skin. You are like the Beatrice painted by Dante Gabriel Rossetti."

Again I blushed. They had called me "carrots" at school or "marmalade" which had annoyed me and made me hit out and then get into trouble for being bad tempered and 'unladylike'.

I suppose it was a compliment, that he would like to paint me but I suddenly realised that artists sometimes wanted nude models. "No – I couldn't…" I stuttered, stepping back a pace.

He smiled again. "I can imagine your thoughts, young Ophelia. I would want to paint you clothed – like the Ophelia in Rossetti's painting. It was my father who kept hiring dubious models – my mother came into the studio one day and saw…well, you are too young to embarrass. Anyway, he has been banished to London." He moved towards me and took my hand. "Please – dear Beatrice – consider it. Only during my summer vacation from art school. I go back to London in September. I might get killed by a bomb from a Zeppelin, you know and you would never have your portrait painted."

He was only half-joking. I had heard of the Germans' huge gas-filled airships flying over England, carrying airmen and bombs and already some people had been killed or injured.

A distant shout made me remember my duties. "I have to get back and find the girls," I said.

He was still holding my hand. "Promise me, you will think about modelling for me? You must have some time off to recover from my sisters. Your friend Elizabeth called with her mother. She saw one of my portraits and asked if I would paint hers, just head and shoulders." He stared into my eyes and I thought I saw a trace of cunning. "I said I was too busy at the moment. But I have been invited to her birthday picnic."

He had probably meant me to be a little jealous – and I was! "Elizabeth is certainly very pretty." I took my hand away, feeling annoyed.

He laughed. "Yes – just like a china doll. And I don't suppose she swims in the river in her undergarments!" He must have seen my horrified expression because he went on, "Don't worry, your secret is safe with me." He put his hand lightly on my arm but let go as I moved away, not wanting to be thought a flirt. I had to confess I missed the oily warmth of his fingers through my thin muslin blouse. I was telling my-self severely that he must be at least seventeen and I wasn't sixteen until the autumn. "I must go," I said again.

"Please come back," he called after me. "And nearly everyone calls me Ronnie, not Oberon."

I turned round at the door. "Was your mother always a nurse?"

"She was an actress when Father met her. Serious plays – Shakespeare and so on. We had a Governess and a Nursemaid and she went on acting while we lived in London. Last year, she gave up acting and trained as a nurse. Then we left London."

I fodund myself saying, "I want to be an actress," Then I wished I hadn't because he looked so interested and began to follow me to the door.

"I might be able to help you," he said eagerly. "My father has – friends – in the theatre."

"That would be…" I began but I could hear one of the girls screaming. "I must go!"

I turned round, once, and saw Ronnie at the door, looking after me.

CHAPTER 6

I followed the screams to a grove of trees and found the girls climbing up to a tree-house – and the screaming had been just to get me there. Perse was half way up to joining Herme, who called down that she was stuck. I only half-believed her and after asking Perse to help – and she went deaf on me – I tucked my skirts into my bloomers and climbed the tree, using the rough notches and pegs someone had hacked into the bark. My legs are strong from swimming and I soon reached Perse, who climbed like a monkey to join her sister. They were both laughing. I told them they could stay up there for all I cared and I got down, shook the twigs from my hair and clothes, and began to walk towards the house.

To my surprise, they followed me and Perse said, "We never had a governess who could climb a tree."

"I've never known such unruly children before," I snapped. "If you don't behave, I shall leave."

They stared at me through their tangled hair.

To my surprise, tough Perse began to cry. "Don't go, Miss Denning. Sorry about hiding in the maze."

"We like you," Herme joined in.

"I shall have to think about it," I said but I couldn't help smiling when Herme did a rather good cartwheel, her thin legs exposed right up to her knickers. There was something like-able about the terrible sisters, after all, but in the back of my mind, I saw Oberon's teasing amber eyes. Now I had met their brother, I thought I could possibly cope with his sisters.

I found they both read well but they wouldn't settle down to do arithmetic so I went to the impressive grand piano, which Father would love – and accompanied myself as I sang "*Burlington Bertie*". I found them sitting cross-legged, listening – and they clapped! I suggested they joined in singing "*Daisy, Daisy, Give me your Answer Do!*" which they did, except they broke into giggles at the end. I tried to get them to play simple scales but of course, they became bored and wandered off.

I kept thinking of Ronnie as I struggled with the girls. Could I really model for him? And what would his mother say? Or my parents, if they found out?

"I can see you coped extremely well," Mrs. R. said when she came back.

I said nothing about the episode of the tree-house.

I had made the girls wash and had encouraged – no, forced them, to sit in the Nursery – which I now called the Schoolroom – and draw the leaves and flowers I had gathered outside. Herme, of course, had other ideas and found watercolour paints which she splodged liberally on the paper, causing it to curl up. Strangely, the colours she'd chosen blended together to make an interesting abstract shape and she ran to her mother, waving the painting.

"Very nice," Mrs. R said, moving back from the dripping picture. "You will have to show your brother. Have you met Oberon, Miss Denning?"

I found I was blushing again. "Yes," I admitted.

"I hope this wretched war will be over before it's compulsory to join up. He has real talent, they say. As you may know, his father paints portraits and he doesn't entirely approve of Oberon's style of painting."

I was so tired of the girls that it was a relief to be sent home, only to be asked to unpeg Monday's washing from the line. Mother was taking Father to give another music lesson. I helped them harness Tommy, had a drink of home-made lemonade and set to work. Needless to say, Jimmy had gone to play with a friend and Alex was out – but he'd have refused to help anyway with 'women's work'.

It's hard to fold sheets on your own and I was feeling sorry for myself when I heard Jem's voice. She was coming out of our kitchen. We often left the front door unlatched in the day-time and she must have let herself in. "I've just put a present for you from Tod on the table – a posy of moon-daisies and a jar of honey from his bees." She giggled. "He's really gone on you now, Bea. I can't think why!"

Her sunburnt face loomed round the flapping washing and I threw Father's nightshirt over her.

"Oberon Rossiter's just said I'm like a girl in a famous painting," I said.

Jem pulled the shirt off her head and threw it back at me. "Going for the rich boy, are you instead of a farmer's son? Talk about a funny name, too."

She was only half-teasing and I felt a flash of guilt as I was fond of Tod.

"So what's it like to be a nursemaid?" she asked.

I unpegged another sheet. "Help me fold this and I'll tell you. I'm a governess, anyway. Those girls are totally out of hand but I shall get them to obey me even if it kills me."

"Not much good if you're dead! Do you rap their hands with a ruler like Miss Sims did at the village school?"

We folded the sheet between us. "Mrs. R. doesn't believe in corporal punishment." I imitated Mrs. Rossiter's voice, rich and deep and definitely dramatic. "She used to be an actress."

"You told me." Jem unpegged a tablecloth and flung the end at me. "Would you put a word in for me? I don't mean for the stage – but I want to work for the hospital, just to get some practical work done – my Dad disapproves of course and there's plenty to do at home in the holidays – and I know it'll be a battle to get trained as a doctor. This war's awful but it does give me a chance to learn. I don't mind what I do."

"I'll try. But we're young. It might be just folding bandages like they do at the Vicarage"

"Or even emptying piss-pots!" She gave one of her loud laughs. "Where's Alex?"

"I suppose he's gone to see Edwin off on the train. He'd like to go with him if he could. I wish he was old enough. I'm sick of his teasing."

"You're mean! Alex's clever and good-looking and I want to know what he's making in the shed," Jem said. "Why don't we look?"

"He'll go mad again!" Then I thought, why not try again now he was safely out of the way. "All right."

We went outside and I noticed that Alex had put a wire sticking out of the top of the shed. I ignored the KEEP OUT notice and opened the door. In the light coming through one window I saw a litter of boxes, tools, a pile of books and pamphlets and a strange contraption made of metal and wires, sitting on a shelf near the door.

"I wonder what it is?" Jem said.

As she spoke, I heard the creaky side door into the garden give a bang and the sound of bicycle wheels. "He's back!" I whispered. "Let's creep out."

But it was too late.

Alex burst into the shed. "Get out!" he yelled. Then he saw Jem. "Taddy knows this is private. She shouldn't have brought you in here."

I felt angry. Alex's hand was on my shoulder, gripping hard.

Jem gave one of her big smiles. She was almost as tall as Alex and moved so she stood between us. "I reckon you're right clever, Alex. What are you making?"

"A machine for Morse Code. You girls would never understand if I explained," he added in an irritating voice. "Now get out of my shed." and he pushed us out, none too gently. I thought Jem would defend herself – she'd fought him often enough when we were younger – but she just laughed.

I left the folded washing on the kitchen table and I put Tod's flowers in a vase. The moon-daisies looked fresh from the field but the red poppies drooped.

"Those poppies are wilting already," Jem said. "They die so quickly. I don't think they like being picked."

"Someone's coming," I said.

Hooves on the lane, a clinking of stirrups and then a knocking on our door. It was unusual for a Sunday.

Elizabeth smiled at me from the back of a beautiful bay horse. She was all decked out, side-saddle and wearing a feathered hat. She bent down and handed me a thick white envelope. "It's the invitation to my sixteenth birthday party I told you about – for you and Alex," she said. Then she went rather pink when she saw Jem. "It has to be small, this year, because of the War."

She was lying and Jem knew it. The Drummonds looked down on tenant farmers.

I was suddenly angry. "You should have brought Jem and Tod's invitation to save a journey to the farm." I knew she had no intention of doing any such thing.

She looked away. "As I said, it's just a small picnic, this year."

"We're too busy for parties anyway." Jem snapped.

I was sick of this new Elizabeth, with all her airs and graces – she'd known Jem and Tod all her life and she had often come to the farm when she was younger – just to enjoy sliding down the straw-stacks with us.

"Unless you invite my friends I will be unable to attend." I thought I sounded amazingly grown-up and I stared at Elizabeth until she looked away.

"You've just heard Jem say they are too busy," she said. "But I shall send round an invitation all the same, to please you, Bea. I tell you who's coming – Oberon Rossiter. I met him with Mama when we called on them. He paints portraits, like his father and he said he might paint mine! He rather liked

36

me, I could tell. Do you know him?"

I wanted to hit her. "Of course I know him – from my first day as a governess. He thinks I look like a famous portrait of Ophelia."

Elizabeth gave me a cold look and said she had other invitations to deliver.

When she had ridden off, Jem started to laugh and I giggled too – so much that we were clinging together in the hall when we heard Tommy and the governess cart coming back and Jem went home.

CHAPTER 7

All that week, I looked forward to going to the Rossiters every day just because I might see Ronnie. The girls played me up all the time but I did get them interested in making a little garden. The Rossiters had kept on one old gardener, Mrs. Maggs' husband, but the younger gardeners had left to join the Army. I bribed old Maggs with some of Mother's scones and home-made jam and he grudgingly allowed Perse and Herme to dig a small plot at the end of a wildly overgrown flowerbed.

I asked him – very nicely – if he would watch and advise the girls on their planting and digging and let them plant seedlings from the greenhouse. It was the only part of the garden he could manage now, together with feeding the white doves who cooed in the dovecot, near the stables.

I slipped away to the studio. I had to find out what Ronnie thought of Elizabeth. Did he really want to paint her portrait? As I stood at the door the music was playing but this time it sounded like dance music but not like the waltzes we'd skated to last winter.

This was modern music – perhaps the Bunny Hug or the Charleston, dances I'd only heard about.

I suddenly felt nervous and I couldn't see Ronnie.

"It's me – Beatrice!" My voice sounded too loud.

He came running, dripping paint off the end of his brush. "Beatrix the Beautiful!" he said, smiling. "Have you thought again about letting me paint you?"

Nobody had ever called me beautiful before. Jem would have said he was buttering me up so I could be an unpaid model but he had such an open look. "What would your mother say? After all, I'm paid to be with the girls. They're busy at the moment but I can't stay long."

"Mama's so obsessed with trying to reorganise the Manor Hospital and having fights with the Matron that she'll never notice. You could come just for an hour at a time."

"I can't just leave them. Besides, your sisters would tell her."

He had his free hand on my shoulder and was gently propelling me towards a couch near his easel. I should be angry, at his taking such liberties – but suddenly, my legs were powerless.

"Just sit there a moment, please," he asked, giving me a pleading look.

My legs felt strangely weak as I sat down.

He stood back, and looked at me through the frame of his fingers. "What time do you leave here?"

"At six. If your mother hasn't returned Mrs. Maggs gives the girls their supper."

"And I know my mama often stays at the hospital until seven or later. So you could just come here for an hour – or less, if you prefer. Tell your parents you are working late."

"I can't lie to them."

"But you will be working – for me! Please, dearest Beatrix, put your feet up on the couch so your skirt falls in folds." In a minute, he had a sketch pad and pencil.

"The girls may come to look for me," I protested.

"They're forbidden here on pain of death. They're scared of the snake."

Immediately I sat up, gathering my skirts. "What snake?"

He laughed. "Please, please relax, dear Beatrix. When we arrived here, I kept a harmless snake as a pet. My terrible sisters don't know it escaped while I was in London. Poor Desdemona – I fear Mr. Maggs may very well kill her on sight." He put his pencil out in front of me, staring at my legs until I blushed and pulled my skirt down over my ankles.

"I'm only measuring, please don't worry." His smile made his thin face glow.

"But…" I began feebly.

"Shall I paint Elizabeth Drummond instead of you?" His voice was teasing but there was just a chance he might paint her.

I weakened. "I shall try to come to your studio – but not every evening."

"Wonderful!" Then he looked rather cast down. "I'm afraid as a student I have little money."

I almost shouted out, "I don't want to be paid!"

"Then you will have to look forward to the time when your portrait is admired by many – in a London gallery."

"London," I muttered. It seemed a far-off dream. "Aren't you scared of going back there, in case there are Zeppelin bombing raids?"

He put the sketch-book down and stared at me almost fiercely. "Scared? When there are men only a year older than me, going to fight in stinking trenches, facing death every day? Coming back blind, without limbs, coming back so shocked by gunfire they call out for their mothers in the night. My mother has talked to me when the girls are in bed. She's been so affected by the sights in the hospital that she can't sleep."

This was a new, serious Ronnie and he made me feel guilty. I had hated the war because it could disturb my life but it had given me the opportunity to work for the Rossiters. We'd heard recently about the sinking of the Lusitania and all the lives lost, Americans as well as English but it had seemed so far away from our village. And everyone said the war would be over by Christmas.

"My father's against the war but my brother Alex wants to enlist as soon as he's old enough. I think he's hoping the war will go on for years."

He frowned. "Selina – my mama, is totally opposed to the war. She says it's a criminal folly and a waste of life and I agree. She wants me to become a Conscientious Objector – a Pacifist but I believe they are often sent to prison. You will think less of me, Beatrix, but I've a confession to make – I hate confined spaces. There were two bully boys at my boarding school and they shut me into a cupboard in our cricket pavilion. I was there for hours."

I found myself getting up and moving towards him, putting my hand on his shoulder, wanting to comfort him. "That was horrible, Ronnie," I said quietly.

He drew me closer. "My father – made me go there because it was his school. I found out he hated it just as much."

"I'm so sorry," I said. Then I felt his arms round me and he was kissing my hair, kissing my face, butterfly kisses, wonderful kisses. "You are a quite amazing girl," he said softly.

He smelled of turpentine, oil paint and his own, slightly musky, man's smell. A strange warmth started low down and spread all over me, tingling. I was filled with an unfamiliar longing.

Then I heard familiar screams in the garden and I broke away from him. "I have to go. It's probably nothing but your sisters might have hurt themselves."

He called after me, "Tell them their brother will be after them with the snake if they don't behave!"

My heart thudded as I ran down to the overgrown kitchen-garden. What if one of them was really hurt? I should never have left them alone again.

The screams increased as I drew nearer to the garden shed. Mr. Maggs had pinned them against the shed wall and was spraying them with a garden hose, turned full on. Was it a game? Then I saw his red, angry face.

"What are you doing?" I called. "Stop at once."

41

He turned the hose off but shouted, "They took my flowers, dug up my chrysanths my dahlias and some of my carrots to plant them in their garden. They broke the stem of my prize marrow. They're the most spoilt selfish little brats and I hope they end up in prison!"

The girls rushed up to me, soaked and crying. "He's gone quite mad!" said Perse.

"We was planting those things in our garden," Herme said. "He's HORRIBLE."

I pushed them away. "I'm not sorry for you. It's Mr. Maggs' job to grow plants. He had every right to be angry." I made them apologise to the old gardener but also told Mr. Maggs off for taking such drastic action but of course all the time I knew it was my fault for leaving them with him.

For the next few days I kept the girls busy with long walks with the dogs, when we gathered leaves and wild-flowers, climbing stiles and pushing through woods until they were really tired – I have to say I was exhausted too because they both talked non-stop. Then they were glad to sit down and write stories from ideas I suggested, about dragons and Princesses, with wild and colourful illustrations. Then we'd press the flowers and leaves into a book. I lured them to the piano by playing and singing myself and they joined in raggedly but at least they tried.

I even took them to the farm at milking time but we left the dogs behind as the Masons had a couple of sheepdogs for their small flock.

"I didn't know milk came like that." Herme stared at the milk squirting between Jem's fingers. Herme laughed at her but I guess she didn't know much about the country either, having been brought up in London until only a few months ago.

Jem showed them the butter-churn but there was something subdued about her. Could she have guessed I was getting fond of Ronnie?

"Where's Tod?" I asked. "I'd hoped to show Star to the girls but her paddock is empty."

Jem's head was pressed into the cow's flank and her words indistinct." He's taking her to another field, much further from the house."

I was glad in a way not to see Tod because I felt guilty about him. I was fond of him – but like a brother and he had scared me, asking if I would marry him one day.

"Well, then they can see the carthorses. I suppose you've brought them in because of the flies."

"There's only old Bess for ploughing now. Davie and Goliath have gone." Jem's voice was muffled and she was crying. They've been taken by the Army. Just right for pulling gun-carriages, the officer said."

"They just took them?" I couldn't believe it. I'd often watched the pair pulling the plough and later, the harvest wagon and I'd admired their gleaming coats, their carefully groomed white fetlocks and their big gentle faces.

"They soft-soaped Da – said it was for our heroic fight against the enemy and gave him five guineas. But we'll not find another pair – other farms have lost their horses. The officer said Bess was too old. This damn war!" She picked up a stick and began to hit out at a patch of nettles as if she'd like to kill that Army officer.

The girls stared at her, open-mouthed.

"What about Star?" I asked.

"That's why he's moved her. The field's surrounded by trees and he's building a shed. We lied to that officer, said we only had the farm horses and Tod had hidden the saddle."

"I'm very sorry." As I said them, the words seemed totally inadequate. "Tod must be so upset about the horses. Are you both coming to Elizabeth's party? It might cheer you up."

"It won't but we're coming – just to show we're as good as those stuck-up Drummonds. All right, they own our farm but we do all the work. I hope their horses have gone too."

"Horrible Army," Herme said as we walked back.

"Horrible War," Perse said and I agreed with her.

I knew I was succeeding with the girls, making them like and obey me and this lessened the guilt I felt telling my parents I was having to work late. Occasionally Mrs. Rossiter would come back by six but I usually left the girls having tea with Mrs. Maggs, I'd ride down the drive as if going home, then hide my bicycle in the bushes and creep back through the garden to the studio.

I wondered sometimes if I were turning into one of those Loose Women. Ronnie began each painting session with a kiss which set me on fire but he was too eager to get to work for my liking.

His artist father had left behind a chest full of shimmering backcloths and exotic clothes and Ronnie found me a glorious dark green silk dress with a full skirt and tight bodice embroidered with tiny daisies. He put up a screen and I went behind it to change – then he brushed out my hair as I sat on the couch, bending over me with a tender expression. The studio must once have been a high-roofed stable and the couch on its raised dais was under a skylight so sunlight shafted through it.

"Your hair is amazing," Ronnie murmured. "It fizzles with light, like a fiery halo round your head. Could you half-shut your eyes and look up slightly."

Then he set to work, holding a handful of brushes and a big palate as he attacked the canvas – I say attacked – because he was no gentle dabbler of paint.

"Please – let me see it," I asked at the end of the week.

Each day he had turned the canvas round, so I couldn't see it.

"Wait till it's finished," he'd say. Then we would kiss, each time holding each other closer. I could feel his hard, lean body pressing into my softness which sent me into a wild imagining that we lay on a romantic grassy bank, under the moon, stroking and holding each other until dawn.

He would gently push me away after a few minutes.

"I wish…" I began

"I know. So do I. But you're only fifteen. I have to take care of you."

A cloud of doves rose from the Cot, very white against the blue sky, and I felt they were exploding into that azure sky to celebrate my love for Ronnie.

Dante and Tara sat sentinel outside the studio. Dante got up and came to me, wagging all over while Tara stared watchfully.

As I stroked the dog, doubt came. Supposing Ronnie was like his father? After all, I was virtually a servant to the Rossiters and I had heard enough stories of servant girls being seduced by their employers or their sons. Expecting a child, they would be dismissed and very probably disowned at home so they ended up in the workhouse or worse.

Mrs. Rossiter had agreed I should take some hours off for Elizabeth Drummond's birthday party. "I was surprised to hear that Ronnie wishes to go," she said. "He's rather shy, I fear, hiding in the studio all day. When you have lived here longer – perhaps you will introduce him to your friends, Miss Denning. I expect you have met him in the grounds when he's walking the dogs."

Had she guessed or was she testing me in some way? I cursed the way I blushed so easily. "Yes, I've met him." I said primly.

Now she was asking me to make sure he enjoyed the party. I suppose I shouldn't have been surprised at her modern way of behaving – but all I had read and heard of a governess working for rich people was that they were looked down upon as socially inferior.

"Of course I'll make sure he knows everyone," I said. Then I remembered Jem's request. This would be a good moment to ask Mrs. Rossiter if she could help the wounded soldiers.

"My friend, Jem Mason from Berry Farm will be there with her brother Tod. She hopes to become a doctor, if she can overcome her father's objections. She'd very much like to work some hours at the Manor Hospital. Would it be possible for you to put in a word with Lady Drummond on Jem's behalf? She's clever, hard-working and reliable."

"Would she mind doing menial work? Emptying chamber-pots, scrubbing floors, changing bed-linen?"

"I'm sure she'd manage. She works very hard on the farm."

Mrs. Rossiter took off her nurse's cap, loosened the high white collar and shook out her bobbed hair. "That's better. The uniform is so hot in this weather. If your friend Jem is only your age, she might find the sights and smells too much. We have had deaths, too. I shall talk to Matron. Lady Drummond merely gives them the use of the West wing of the Manor. She doesn't run the hospital personally."

I thanked her and went home but I wasn't thinking about Jem, only of the party and what I should wear. I had so few clothes and Elizabeth was sure to wear a new outfit.

I wanted Ronnie's eyes to glow as they did in the studio, so everyone could see he was fond of me.

Then, I thought of Tod. How would he feel?

CHAPTER 8

I put off trying on clothes until Saturday morning when Mother was out, taking Father to a music pupil in the next village. She had promised to drive me to the lake, where the picnic was to be held if the weather was fine.

Elizabeth was lucky – it was hot again, so hot that I longed to swim in the river.

What to wear? The choice was simple – I could wear one of my three Sunday best blouses, high-necked and prim, with the dark blue poplin skirt Mother had made me last year. I thought of Mrs. Rossiter's dashing clothes – mine were so old-fashioned.

Then I thought of the old trunk in the attic where Mother kept scarves and shawls from the past, when she lived at home in a big house and went to grand parties, before she married Father.

Alex was in his shed and Jimmy out playing with a village lad.

Nobody would disturb me. I lit a lamp and climbed the steep stairs, pushing open the trap-door with one hand.

The trunk was dusty and when I opened it, the clothes smelled of mothballs and old lavender.

I found a Christening robe, wrapped in tissue paper, several shawls, too warm for summer, then, carefully wrapped in more paper, was a kingfisher-blue silk dress. I took it downstairs and tried it on in front of Mother's long mirror.

It was a little big on me – Mother must have worn it when

she was older and had bigger breasts than me – but I loved the set-in long puffed sleeves and the fullness of the skirt. I knew it was the cut was old-fashioned but the colour was amazing and seemed to bring out the brightness of my hair, which I planned to wear loose, as Ronnie liked it. I just needed to go over it with a cloth and the flat-iron.

Everyone would stare at me and Ronnie would love it.

"Bea – dearest!" Mother exclaimed as I came downstairs in the afternoon. "That's my old dress. You look – lovely – but it isn't suitable for a picnic. I wore it for my first dance."

"Do you mind my wearing it?" I asked, twirling round.

"No – but I think you would be much better in your white blouse and dark skirt."

"Please Mother! I'm so tired of my own clothes."

"You'll have to learn to make your own dresses, as I do," she said with a sigh. "I think you have made a wrong decision, Beatrice. At least wear your hat to keep off the sun."

"No thank you." I had brushed my hair until it gleamed and I wanted Ronnie to see it like that.

It was unfortunate that Alex came along just as I was following Mother into the governess cart. "Going to a ball, Taddy?" and he laughed. "I might look in at the party later on. I would hate to disappoint the fair Elizabeth. I want to know if she's had news of Edwin since he went back."

I swished past him with what I hoped was a haughty look and nearly tripped as I climbed into the cart.

Alex laughed. "How very suitable for a Governess to arrive in a Governess Cart! But you should dress more demurely, Bea." Then he walked away.

Mother sighed. "Some boys would be pleased to escort their sisters but not Alex." She flapped the reins on Tommy's back and he trotted slowly along the road. I did wish we could arrive in a smart trap, or carriage – or even better, a motor-car – but there it was, we were poor. It would have been better if I could have driven myself but Mother was taking Father to give a piano lesson. Now I was alone on one of the seats behind Mother – like a child being taken to a party.

The lake was in a distant part of the Manor's many acres and approached by a narrow lane, now crowded with smart traps and carriages. Behind us, I heard a motor-car. Would Mrs. Rossiter bring Ronnie?

There was an open gate into a field just before the wood which surrounded the lake and I saw grooms leading horses and traps into the shade, presumably to wait for the return journey. I was already ashamed of old Tommy's sagging back and our battered cart and now Mother was insisting on collecting me. I'd had some vague idea Mrs. Rossiter might offer me a lift and I would sit next to Ronnie…

By the time we arrived by the newly mowed grass by the lake, I was sweating under the hot sun and wished I was wearing my straw hat. The Drummonds' servants had erected a pretty silken tent. A damask cloth covered a long table, on which were all kinds of cakes and sandwiches and the big birthday cake, iced with pink roses and green leaves. Two decorated rowing-boats were tied up by the water.

Lady Drummond sat in a wicker chair, directing the proceedings in a commanding voice, the pink flowers on her big straw hat twitching as she moved her head from side to side, checking that all was in order.

Groups of girls giggled and talked together as they drank glasses of fruit cup, while the boys were in a group, larking about, pretending to push each other into the water.

After Mother had driven off, I stood there, wishing I had gone back with her. All the girls were wearing light, flowery summer dresses, pretty straw hats and the latest strap slippers. I knew at once my long dress was quite wrong for a picnic and definitely old-fashioned and I was wearing my old and scuffed indoor shoes.

It was oppressively hot and the dark trees surrounding the lake seemed to trap the heat, their tops perfectly reflected in the still water. It seemed much more than six months ago when we skated on the lake, that first Christmas of the war, when we all thought it would soon be over. I loved dancing on ice and Tod had been my partner to the Blue Danube waltz, played on the gramophone. Alex, of course, tore round the lake, doing figures-of-eight and scaring the more timid skaters. Later, he danced with Elizabeth. Servants had lit candles and slow-burning torches round the water and I'd see Elizabeth stumble – I guess on purpose – and cling on to Alex, who held her very close.

Now, there she was, dressed in pale blue linen. "So glad you could come, Beatrice," she said, looking me up and down. "Where did you find that gown?" she asked. "Lovely colour but you may find it rather hot."

"I am perfectly cool, thank you," I lied and I gave her the present I had bought – a carved wooden box made by Silas Wainwright, a carpenter and distant cousin.

She undid the silk ribbon and unwrapped the tissue paper. "How perfectly charming. What is it for?"

"There's a lock and key. You can keep your love-letters in it," I said in a bright but rather unpleasant voice.

"Oh – look, there's the Rossiters' motor-car!" She ran forward to greet them.

Ronnie would be sure to find her captivating – cool in her summer dress whereas I was so hot I could feel sweat trickling down my back in a most unladylike way.

Then I felt a light tap on my shoulders. "Beatrix" he said softly. "That colour is amazing on you."

Before I could reply, Elizabeth almost ran to us, ignoring me. "Oberon! I'm so very glad you could come. I knew you'd appreciate such an artistic scene. Let me introduce you to some of my friends."

She had the cheek to take his arm and almost drag him away. I was staring angrily after them when I heard a motor-cycle's roar.

Everyone turned to look as Tod zoomed onto the grass, with Jem on the back riding astride, of all things.

He stopped so abruptly that she almost fell off. The journey had blown Jem's thick hair on end and she was wearing the latest cycling bloomers.

She strode over. "He's only come because he can see you," she snapped.

I saw Tod self-consciously shaking the dust off his jacket and looking at me. I went up to him, smiling. I hated to see him so ill at ease.

He looked at me. "I like the colour of your dress, Bea."

I felt divided. Here was poor Tod, so fond of me, and there was Ronnie, standing close to Elizabeth while she showed him off to her friends almost as if he were her sweetheart.

I was tempted and gave way. A nasty little worm in my brain told me if I chatted happily to Tod, Ronnie might be jealous. Jem was showing the motor-bike off to a couple of lads. I felt ashamed of myself even as I did it, linking my arm in Tod's and taking him off to the tent where I plied him with fruit cup and dainty cucumber sandwiches, arranged on silver trays. "Far too small," He smiled as he ate three at once and then I saw he had not been able to get all the dust and grease out of his hands and nails.

I felt pity and shame for him which I stifled with a flow of bright chatter. Then I remembers his sadness about the horses. "Is Star still all right?" I asked.

"So far. I'm just fearful the Army will come back for her." He took my arm and pulled me out of the crowded tent. "Let's walk along the lakeside. I have such happy memories of skating here with you," but we had only gone a few yards when sharp-eyed Lady Drummond called, "No escaping, please. We are going to light the candles and then take the boats out."

So we had to walk back. I saw Ronnie looking at me and I pulled my hand out of Tod's firm grasp.

51

We were asked to sit down while a servant brought out the cake and lit its sixteen candles, whose flame didn't waver in the ominously still air. I noticed a black cloud had covered the sun and it felt as if there might be a storm brewing.

Elizabeth made a great fuss of blowing out the candles and cutting the cake while everyone clapped and some sang Happy Birthday. "Wish, wish!" someone called as she cut. She was looking directly at Ronnie as she plunged the silver knife into the pink icing so it didn't take much brain power to know what she was wishing.

A servant handed the cake round on a silver salver and then the boys hurried to the boats, leaping on so even the steady punts rocked.

"Are you coming, Bea?" Jem asked. "I'm going to ask to row, if they'd let a mere girl have a go."

"How about it, Bea?" Tod asked.

I saw Ronnie, further down the bank saying something to Elizabeth, so she turned back, frowning. He waved at me.

Tod saw him.

"There's going to be a storm – it's giving me a headache," I said.

Tod guessed what I really felt and walked away with Jem. I knew I must have hurt him.

Jem spoke angrily over her shoulder. "Run after that foppish artist, Bea!" she said. "What do old friends matter when you're after a rich boyfriend."

There were shrieks and giggles all round as the girls got into the boats and I pretended I hadn't heard her, as I walked to join Ronnie.

He took my arm. "Let's get away for a moment while they're all on the lake," he said urgently. "Unless you want to join your other admirer." He looked pointedly at Tod.

I felt a pang of sadness. Why couldn't Tod accept we were good friends, like a brother and sister? Elizabeth was being helped into one of the boats but she turned round and stared directly at us. I couldn't help being pleased that Ronnie preferred my company to hers. She was so spoilt that she probably thought she could attract any boy she chose.

"Ronnie – I've known Tod and Jem Mason all my life." I still felt a traitor but Ronnie holding my hand made me almost dizzy with delight.

We left the noisy crowd behind as we walked towards the other end of the lake. "I wish we could be together like this all the time," he said.

I quite forget to be demure and not too willing. "Yes," I said, leading him to a log, carved into a seat and decorated by a woman's head, wearing a crown of leaves, which wove round the whole seat with the words flowing from her mouth.

"I call her the Green Lady," I said.

Ronnie read out loud; *"Life is good. Live gently, with fire and always with hope."*

"That's wonderful!" he said. "I don't know about living gently but certainly one should live with fire."

"Our cousin carved it for the Drummonds, some time ago," I said. "Shall we sit here?"

We sat close together, holding hands. "I hate the thought of going back to art school in London and not seeing you." He kissed me lightly on the forehead and stroked my hair. Even his touch made me feel as if I were on fire.

Then I had an idea. " You know I want to become an actress and your parents know all sorts of artistic and theatrical people, don't they?"

He laughed. "My father is more or less living with a music hall actress. I'm not supposed to tell anyone."

I felt excited. "Is she famous?"

"Bunny Delgardo."

"I've heard of her! She's almost as famous as Vesta Tilley or Marie Lloyd." I'd read reviews of their performances in Father's newspaper and I remembered every word. "Perhaps you could get me an introduction – I know I can't train now but…"

His arm crept round my waist so we leaned together and whispered, "Oh, I do wish you could come to London with me!"

We looked at each other knowing it was almost impossible, at least until I was older. And who knows what pretty art student might have taken his fancy by then?

I was startled by a clap of thunder and a few drops of rain. "We'd better hurry back – the storm's coming." Why were we always interrupted?

We were running back as the lightning flickered across the water. As we drew near, I saw Elizabeth standing up in one of the boats, her pale dress fluttering and then she overbalanced and fell in with a shriek.

Her arms churned and she called out something. The others shouted but did nothing.

"She told me she can't swim – we'll have to help," I said. Ronnie stripped off his trousers and dived into the lake. I pulled off my dress, kicked off my shoes and jumped in after him, thankful I wasn't wearing a corset to impede my progress. I didn't like Elizabeth but I didn't want her to drown and supposing Ronnie knew little of life-saving? As I swam I felt the thick water-weed clinging to my feet and I remembered the stable-boy who drowned in the lake.

Ronnie was trying to hold Elizabeth when I came up and the boat looked as if it might tip over, with all its crew leaning over, waving paddles and a punting pole for her to grasp.

"Stop struggling!" I shouted at her but immediately she tried to hold me round the neck so I slapped her face, hard. She cried out, let me go and I managed to hold her under the shoulders, while swimming strongly on my back towards the bank. Ronnie swam alongside, firmly holding her flailing arm and shouting at her to keep still.

We dragged her onto land just as the boats came in and we

were surrounded by a crowd of guests and servants, who fell back as Lady Drummond came running, and Elizabeth fell into her arms, crying and coughing out lake-water. Her pretty dress was sticking wetly to her corset and I wanted to giggle but I was suddenly conscious of my own wet underwear clinging to me and Ronnie wearing only his drawers. We had no time to fetch our clothes because another thunderclap seemed almost to announce a sweating, nervous horse bearing a servant wearing the Drummond livery. He dismounted and someone held the horse while he came up to Lady Drummond and gave her a brown envelope.

Lightning illuminated her face while she opened it.

She gave a terrible cry and fainted at our feet.

CHAPTER 9

Soon the whole village had heard the news that Edwin Drummond had been killed. Alex took the news very badly and disappeared for a whole day – we had no idea where he went.

I had been saddened by the deaths at the battle of Mons earlier in the year of those young men from Lower Thane, the next village, but I hadn't known them. It was so hard to believe that arrogant, good-looking Edwin was dead. Before he went away to school we'd all played together, damming streams and fishing for tiddlers, even making a rough hut in the woods. I decided that was the Edwin I would remember.

There was a funeral at the village church to commemorate Edwin's life. It was strange, a funeral without a coffin. I overheard one of the young officers from his Regiment whisper to another, "There wasn't anything left of him to bury."

The Vicar spoke of Edwin's heroic sacrifice to defend his country and added, "All able-bodied young men should follow his example."

Sir Pelham Drummond, wounded in the Boar War, was supported by his manservant as the family went up the aisle. I was pumping the organ but I could just see Elizabeth, deadly pale and thin in her black dress.

The Masons were Chapel and did not come. I would have liked to see Jem and try to make amends for neglecting Tod but I heard that she had started work for a few hours each evening at the hospital.

A few days after the funeral, I went to the studio to sit for Ronnie but found him pale and distracted. "I can't paint today, Bea." He came up to me, and held me close so I could feel his heart beating fast. "Someone has sent me one of those white feathers."

I had heard of the white feather campaign, started by some stupid old Admiral, telling girls and women to hand white feathers to those young men they thought should enlist. Father had become quite angry saying the whole affair was criminal and cruel.

Now I held Ronnie in my arms. "You mustn't take any notice. It's some stupid woman who doesn't know you are a student. Please, please take no notice."

"I don't believe wars solve anything. Selina – my mother – is a pacifist but.."

"Please, Ronnie. You have to stick to what you believe is right." I began to cry. "I couldn't bear it if you went to the Front. You could get killed or horribly wounded. Promise you won't take any notice of that white feather."

I was trembling by then and he stroked my hair and my shoulders. "All right, for your sake I'll try, my darling Beata Beatrix – and it wasn't given to me, but sent by post in a thick white envelope. We'll forget all about it and go back to the portrait."

I lay back on the couch, the flower in my hand, my hair spread over the cushion and my eyes closed. Ronnie said he had almost finished my head and shoulders portrait and now he wanted to portray me as Millais, the pre-Raphaelite artist, would have done. "Not my style," he said. "But I want to try something different."

He still refused to show me either work.

I sat back on the couch and tried to relax but I kept thinking of Edwin being 'blown to bits' and worrying that this sick person who sent the white feather might make Ronnie feel guilty.

When the hour was up, he came to lie beside me on the couch and took me in his arms. All thoughts of war melted away as we kissed. I could feel that he wanted me as much as I wanted him but he moved away, breathing fast.

"You're too young. It wouldn't be fair to seduce you, especially as I love you, Bea."

"I love you too," I began and then the dogs barked, silenced at once by a voice I knew.

Ronnie's mother strode into the studio as I was hastily re-arranging the embroidered gown.

"Beatrice! What are you doing here and dressed like that?" Her face was pale and angry.

"It's my fault, Selina," Ronnie said quickly. "I asked Beatrice to sit for me. Her hair is ideal for a pre-Raphaelite painting. Don't blame her, blame me – I persuaded her to stay on after work."

"Mrs. Maggs said you left the house at six. I don't like lies, Beatrice. And Ronnie, you are old enough to know better. I hope you are not taking after your father," she added in a low voice.

So that was it. Mrs. Rossiter would send me off without a reference and she might even tell Father.

"I'm sorry." I found I was crying as I went to the screen and changed into my ordinary clothes. All the time I could hear mother and son arguing in low voices, too low for me to hear.

As I ran out of the studio, Mrs. Rossiter called my name.

But I couldn't go back.

I found my hidden bicycle and peddled fast, crying so much I could hardly see. I felt I couldn't go home – Mother would see my face and try to find out what had happened, so I cycled to the farm to see Jem.

In my misery, I had forgotten she would be going to the hospital later on.

"We're having our tea," she said when she came to the door. "I can't ask you in because I have to hurry to the hospital.

What's the matter, Bea?"

I remembered Tod. I couldn't tell her I loved Ronnie and Mrs. R. had found out – instead I blurted out, "Ronnie Rossiter's had a white feather sent him. He's talking of enlisting."

She grabbed my arm so hard in her strong fingers that it hurt. "Tod's had one too – by post. Your Alex came round and they went off together – he's missed his tea and left the fence he was mending." Then Jem, my tough friend, was crying too. "They found out about Star – left us twenty pounds and took her today. Tod's that upset. The white feather just tipped him over. I couldn't bear to see him so unhappy – first about you and that Ronnie – now this."

What could I say? Jem was my best friend – I had to help her but I felt so guilty. Tod had an extra reason to enlist – after I'd hurt him. "I'm so sorry – I didn't mean – but I do love Ronnie.." it all spilled out in a muddle between my sobs.

Then Jem suddenly hugged me, so hard she almost crushed my ribs. She smelled of onions and cows but I didn't care. Perhaps she could forgive me. "Mam's calling me back for my tea. I have to go." She looked down at me – big strong Jem, broken enough to say, "What can we do?"

"I don't know," was all I could say.

"It's your Alex too, you know. I heard him tell Tod that some bitch had sent him a white feather."

"We'd not stop him going. He's been longing to enlist."

And did I want my tiresome, bullying brother at home? Life would be peaceful, without him. I tried to banish that thought by remembering Edwin's being 'blown to bits.'

"Your Ronnie won't go to war," Jem said scornfully. "He'll be too sensitive and scared." Then she went, shutting the door in my face.

How could I be best friends when she made a remark like that? And yet we had hugged each other and I was so sorry for Tod.

I dried my face and went home.

CHAPTER 10

Alex didn't come back that evening. Mother found a note, half-hidden on the mantelshelf. He'd taken a rucksack, boots and underclothes.

"I am off to enlist – perhaps with Tod if he wants. I want to get at those evil Huns and I'm not staying here to be called a coward. Sorry – and my love to you all. Alex."

"There's something in the envelope." Mother shook out a white feather, which curled its way to the ground.

Jimmy marched up and down with his stick on his shoulder. "I wish I could go and fight too."

"They'll be sent back, under age," Father said when he heard.

I knew Alex would get round that with one of his clever lies.

I couldn't go back to the Rossiters after what had happened and yet I had to make sure Ronnie wouldn't want to follow Alex and Tod. I tossed and turned all night, falling asleep just at dawn. It seemed a moment later when I was woken by a knocking on the front door.

Jem stood there, wearing her sacking apron. "Tod came back for his things. He wouldn't listen to my Da – he said he'd follow his horses and Alex was waiting for him but he wouldn't say where. It's all your Alex's fault. Tod would have laughed off that white feather. Now I've got to get back to the milking. We're a man short for all the work."

And she marched off, her big boots clacking on the cobbles.

So she preferred to blame Alex, rather than Tod's being

upset about the horses and getting the white feather.

"You're not dressed, Bea. Won't you be late for work?" Mother asked when she found me standing there, unable to move because I didn't know what to do.

I couldn't tell her of my disgrace. Later, perhaps, when she was used to Alex being away. I couldn't eat breakfast.

My mind churned round as I got out my bicycle. Who had sent the feathers? Would Ronnie keep his promise to me and refuse to enlist?

I cycled aimlessly, wondering what to do. Where could I hide all day? The thunderstorm had broken the heat wave and grey clouds rolled over the sky, promising rain. Automatically, I had ridden towards Tanglemere and as I slowed down, wondering miserably whether the girls would miss me, Mrs. Rossiter's car came out of the drive.

I nearly fell off as she stopped with a screech of brakes and a hooting of the horn. I wanted to run away but she jumped out and confronted me. "I was coming to see you, Miss Denning" She was severe in her nurse's uniform, the starched cap making her seem very tall and frightening.

"Please don't tell my parents," I was crying again.

"The girls are missing you. Ronnie has sworn it was entirely his fault and he will not use you as a model again. I can see my son put you in a compromising position." She put out a leather–gloved hand and touched my arm. "In any event, he seems bent on enlisting. He will be eighteen in two weeks' time and then does not need his parents' consent."

"I could persuade him to stay," I said in a low voice, knowing I was being presumptuous.

She looked at me. "If you could…"

"My brother and his friend have just run off to the Army," I blurted out. "Someone sent them white feathers, like Ronnie."

Her face flushed with anger. "I was disgusted when he told me. Such people should be publicly shamed. If they could see the wounded – a young man of eighteen blinded – another with stumps for arms and infection spreading. Your friend Jem is so young to see such terrible sights." She sighed. "I have to get to the hospital. Beatrice – if you want I will have you back. The girls like you and I know I won't find anyone else in a hurry." She smiled. "That sounds rude. No, I'm please with your work but please do not go to the studio."

"Thank you." I couldn't believe it. I had heard tales of girls working in big houses, seduced by the son of the house, who were dismissed at once. But I reminded myself I hadn't been seduced – yet.

I felt a little guilty when she put her arm round me. "I am so sorry about your brother. I think your father said he was only sixteen. They will send him back. And I think I have made Ronnie see sense. At the moment, he has a choice. If the war goes on, he may have to enlist."

I had to see Ronnie. If only he joined us for lunch but Mrs. Maggs usually took him sandwiches. As I cycled up the drive, I realised I had only promised not to go to the studio – I could see him somewhere else.

Mrs. Maggs gave me a nasty look when I came into the kitchen where the girls were having breakfast. I took no notice and hurried them off into the garden before the rain came, to collect more specimen flowers and leaves for their scrapbooks.

"We've done that. It's boring," Herme said

"I would rather paint," Perse said. She looked at me cunningly. "Ronnie could help us paint, couldn't he, Miss?"

Somehow the girls had guessed where I spent some evenings. I felt myself flush as I wondered if they had followed me and seen us.

All the time I was trying to work out a plan to see Ronnie. Then I felt a pang of dismay. He couldn't be very fond of me if he just obeyed his mother and stayed in the studio. Was he a 'mother's boy' after all?

"Afterwards, you can climb into the tree house unless it

63

rains," I promised recklessly.

I walked with them, picking damp leaves, grasses and the flowers I thought Maggs wouldn't notice. I argued with myself about Ronnie, obeying his mother so easily – but I knew I loved him, whatever he was like.

I kept thinking I heard a slight sound, muted by the girls' chatter – but when I looked round, nobody was there. I hadn't seen the dogs that day so perhaps one of them was following us, nosing into bushes to look for rabbits. Big black crows were cawing to one another from the trees at the end of the garden. One flew over our heads, making Herme cry out.

"Mrs. Maggs says crows mean death," Perse said cheerfully.

"What rubbish!" I laughed but I shivered all the same and wished she had not talked of death. "I think they're rather magnificent birds and I've often wondered what they are cawing about to each other." I shivered, though, remembering Father telling me that a company of the birds was called a 'murder' of crows.

We put our specimens into water until I had time to press and label them, then the girls persuaded me to let them go to the tree-house. I gave way, warning them to be very careful and told them I would be back soon.

I wandered off, keeping near enough to hear the girls if they called out. Soon I would call them in for tea and cycle home. I tried to tell myself that the boys might have come back but I knew how determined Alex could be, so it was unlikely.

I didn't want to face my mother's sadness nor Father's bitter anger.

The Maze was ahead, dark yew against the pale sky. A flash of a white shirt, someone darting into the entrance – my heart beat very fast. It was Ronnie!

I picked up my tiresome skirt and ran fast. By the time I got there, he'd disappeared from the entrance but as soon as I ran into the semi-darkness, his hands reached out and were round my waist in a moment, drawing me inside the protecting walls of yew.

"Darling Beatrix," he whispered. "I've been following you round but my sisters were too close."

His lips tasted faintly of oil-paint as he kissed me and I again felt that fire creeping from deep inside me.

"Your mother..." I began when I could breathe again.

"Yes, yes," he interrupted. "I am so sorry. I should never ...I was carried away...Can you forgive me?"

I stopped his mouth with a lingering kiss. We clung together until I said, "I have to get back to the girls. Please, if you really do love me, don't enlist. Alex and Tod have had white feathers and they went off yesterday."

He moved a little away from me. "Other lads from the Slade have enlisted, joining the Artists Rifles. My mama has told me such tales of the wounded that I would like to help the doctors on the battlefield. That feather made me see it isn't fair to be safe, just painting, while men are suffering so much."

"Your mother thinks war is evil," I reminded him.

"But she's helping nurse the wounded. Anyway, I have told her I shall join her at the hospital to help where I can. It will be practice for me if I enlist. I hear your friend Jem from the farm does menial tasks there in the evenings and I can do the same. I'm strong – I can lift the men, push wheelchairs. And I'm not scared of blood."

"What about your painting?" I was scared when he said 'if I join up'.

"That can wait. By the way, I've finished your portrait."

I hugged him. "I want to see it."

"The paint's not dry yet but if you like, I could bring it to the studio door – so you won't have to come inside."

I followed him as he went to the studio then waited outside until he came.

He held up the canvas.

It was me and yet not me. I remembered his tilting my head

slightly up and telling me to half-close my eyes, as if remembering something amazing – but this made me look strange as he had emphasised my pale skin - and, I was pleased to see, removed the freckles! - and made my hair a darker chestnut. "I look as if I'm dying," I called out. "And why is there a red dove in my lap, holding a red poppy? I hope you didn't kill one of Mr. Maggs' doves for that picture!"

He smiled at me. "I wouldn't dare! No, I've based the painting on a famous one by Mr. Millais – only it is your face, Bea, and the background is quite different and his poppy is white." His voice lowered. "The red dove is dipped in the blood of war and carries the poppy, bringing sleep and death. But you, Beata Beatrix, have overcome..."

I never heard the rest of his art lecture because there was a piercing shriek from the direction of the tree-house. It might be a hoax to gain my attention like the last time but I couldn't risk leaving them. "They may be hurt!" I called and Ronnie put down the painting and we ran fast to the big chestnut tree.

I saw thin legs and arms sawing the air above me – a dead-looking branch had spiked Herme's shift dress and held her, swinging dangerously about fifteen feet from the ground below the wooden platform of the tree-house. Perse had climbed up opposite the branch but couldn't reach her sister. "She fell and the branch caught her up," she gasped, crying. "That branch will break..."

I flung off my hampering skirt and was up, using the hand-holds and Ronnie was beside me, hanging on as best he could. Perse clung to the tree, sobbing, as I stood on the branch just above the revolving Herme.

Ronnie held me close with one arm as I reached out to Herme. "Reach out to me!" I shouted.

She screamed and swung helplessly and the rotten branch creaked.

"Do as you're told!" Ronnie thundered at her and I

66

managed to grasp her hands.

At that moment the branch cracked and Ronnie reached round me to help hold her. For a moment I thought she'd slip out of our grasp but she almost jumped into our arms and somehow we all scrambled down, scratched and out of breath and both girls crying.

Mrs. Rossiter was standing there. She looked at the twigs in my hair and my state of undress. "So what exactly have you been doing?" she asked.

CHAPTER 11

I went home that day but not in disgrace as I'd feared. Perse said I had saved Herme's life – Ronnie said I hadn't been to the studio and Mrs. Rossiter, who looked so angry at first, had thanked me but she forbade the girls to climb to the tree-house until Maggs had made a proper ladder. The girls didn't tell tales, so she never knew I had let them go up on their own.

I refused her offer of tea because I knew I had to get home and find out if there was any news but there was none. Mother was almost angrily slapping down the flat-iron on a sheet and Father was playing Chopin, loudly. I could see they were trying to behave normally, partly for Jimmy's sake, so I went along with Mother when she said she was sure Alex and Tod would be back soon, "Tails between their legs, being too young," she said with a wavering smile. I offered to help with the ironing, which I hated, but she said she needed to keep busy and she was nearly finished.

I wanted to find out who had sent the letters so I went to Alex's room, which had been left as it was, ready for him to return.

He always forbade me to go inside, so I stood there, looking at his untidy shelves and the curious number of things he had collected, animal and bird skeletons, bits of strange machinery, lumps of quartz, to say nothing of the open books on his desk and somehow he had got hold of the poster with the General pointing straight at you and the words
YOUR COUNTRY NEEDS YOU!

Would he have kept the letter? I looked everywhere, disturbing dust and moving his sacred objects. Mother had made his bed but I stripped it. Nothing. Then I looked underneath and saw a white envelope.

I made out from the stamp that the envelope had been posted from our nearest town, Falford, and although the address was printed, there was something familiar about the dark blue ink and the way the letters were formed, with a kind of twiddle on the A and a flourish on the 'q' in 'Esquire'. Alex hardly ever received letters except from rich Aunt Agnes on his birthday, and they were addressed to Master Alexander Denning.

Tod's and Ronnie's letters had come by post, too. I thought I'd heard that men were handed white feathers in the street but this sounded much more deliberate.

Suddenly I knew where I had seen those looping capital letters before and the blue ink. Mother complained that I was untidy and never threw things away – I rummaged in the drawer where I'd kept everything from old schoolbooks and poetry I'd written to hair-ribbons and abandoned attempts to embroider handkerchiefs as Christmas presents.

There it was. A thick white envelope, blue ink, same twiddles – Elizabeth's writing, sending the party invitation.

I found it hard to eat supper and help Mother with the dishes but at last I was free to go out. I told Mother I wouldn't be long and peddled off to see Jem.

"She's just left," her mother said. "Have you any news?" She was a big woman, built like Jem, but she seemed to have shrunk into herself, and her eyes were red-rimmed.

"Sorry – no news," I said and felt very sad as I peddled off to catch up with Jem. Already our house seemed empty without Alex's irritating presence and I couldn't bear to think of gentle, kindly Tod being trained to kill anyone.

I caught up with Jem just as she turned into the Manor gates. When I called her, she stopped. "Oh, it's you," she said in a tired voice. She wore a white overall and her hair was tied back into a white cap.

"I think I've found who sent the white feathers," I said.

"But the damage is done, isn't it?" This was so unlike Jem. I had thought she would want revenge.

"It's Elizabeth Drummond, I'm sure. I'm going there now."

"They're toffs – a privileged lot. Think they can do anything. You won't get her to apologise."

"Come with me."

"I can't. I'm already five minutes late and I promised one of the soldiers I'd take down a letter to his girlfriend."

Jem was already moving away, towards the hospital wing. "Is he illiterate?" I asked because I couldn't think of anything else to say.

"Left his hands on the battlefield, didn't he? And he looks like losing his arms to infection. There must be something better to kill bacteria than disinfectant. I shall find the answer when I'm a doctor."

And she was gone, hurrying towards the hospital.

I stood there, feeling I had lost my best friend.

There was a black wreath on the front door. I pulled at the ancient bell-rope and the old butler, Sims, came to the door. "Sir Pelham and Lady Drummond are not receiving visitors," he said in a voice like a creaky door.

"I've come to see Miss Elizabeth," I said. "It's very important. A matter of life or death."

"I don't know…" he began but a sudden boldness filled me and I literally pushed past the little old man and ran up the wide staircase to Elizabeth's newly decorated room, which she had shown me last Christmas. I burst inside, calling her name.

I suppose I had half expected her to be somewhere else in the great house but there she was, flung down on her pink-draped bed, her black dress rucked up and her thumb in her mouth. She was asleep.

I had been ready to attack her – probably verbally but maybe physically but seeing her like this, made me hesitate. Then I told myself not to be so soft and gave her a prod.

She opened her eyes and gave a little scream, seeing me standing over her.

"You sent white feathers to my brother and to Tod and Ronnie!" I said loudly.

She sat up. Her eyes were almost slits, they were so swollen with tears. "How did you find out?" she whispered.

"Your writing on the envelope. Why did you do it? Alex and Tod have run off to enlist."

Her hands were trembling as she got up and righted her skirt. When she spoke, her voice was trembling too. "I didn't see why they should all be safe at home when Edwin was dead. They should all fight to avenge his death. We've got to kill those horrible Germans…kill, kill kill!" Then she burst into loud hysterical sobs. At any moment her mother or the servants would hear and come running.

I took her arms and shook her. "Be quiet!" I ordered and the sobs diminished. "Do you think Edwin would have wanted you to do this to boys he's known all his life? He was three years older than Alex and Tod. And what have you got against Ronnie?"

She didn't answer but I knew. She had liked him and she was jealous of me.

"Please forgive me!" she whispered and I felt her body crumple up as I held her.

Was she pretending or was she really fainting?

With an effort, because she was fatter than she looked, I propped her on the bed and pushed her head down, between her knees.

At that moment, Lady Drummond burst into the room. "Why are you here, Beatrice? What have you done to her?"

She rushed to her daughter, her corsets creaking as she bent over her. "Hasn't she suffered enough?" she demanded.

Elizabeth suddenly recovered and pushed her mother away.

"It's not her fault. I sent white feathers to Bea's brother and to Tod Mason and Ronnie Rossiter. Two of them have gone to enlist. I was wrong. I don't want them to be killed."

There was a terrible silence in the room.

Then Lady Drummond looked at me, without speaking. Her face was pale and there were dark circles round her eyes. I slid out of the room, suddenly realising what it must be like for her to lose her only son.

As I cycled back I felt even more divided in my mind. I was sad Tod had gone to enlist and I was scared Ronnie would join them – but life would be so much more peaceful without Alex's teasing.

Then that thought made me feel guilty. Alex could be wounded. He could even be killed – although I just couldn't imagine it. He would surely have a charmed life.

But my mind was filled with worry about my darling Ronnie, as I privately called him. How could I stop him going to war?

The boys didn't return. Father said the Army would send them back, because they were under age, but I knew Alex would lie convincingly and be accepted.

One evening, Jem came round after she'd been to the hospital, just to see if we'd had any news. "They won't come back," she said and she burst into tears. "I just sat with a man who was dying. He thought I was his girl and he wanted me to kiss him. I did but the rotting smell was that bad that I threw up and Matron was angry. Suppose Tod – or Alex gets wounded like that."

I began to cry too and we hugged each other, sobbing.

Jimmy and Father had gone to bed but Mother was still up and now she made Jem come and sit in the kitchen and drink sweet tea.

There was a silence, only broken by our three Grandfather clocks striking eleven one after another.

"Your parents will be worried, Jem," Mother said at last and as Jem prepared to leave, Mr. Mason came to the door, a lantern swinging in his hand.

"She said she might call in here – I've been up with a sick cow. I'd a mind to shoot that officer when he came to take Star. Now I want to kill them Generals what started the war. I don't even know what it's all about."

Mother put her hand on his shoulder. "My husband says the army is like a huge animal whose appetite is never satisfied."

Mr. Mason's whole face seemed to change so he looked old and angry. "All I know is that my lad has left me in the lurch to manage on my own," he said. "Our Jem will have to leave that High School and help us out."

I could just see Jem's expression in the flickering light. All her hopes and all her dreams were vanishing. She was both sad and angry.

"I shall still work at the hospital, Dad," she said defiantly. "It's not my fault that Bea's brother persuaded our Tod to go to war." She glared at me.

"Jem…" I began. I'm not sure what I was going to say but already Mr. Mason had her arm and was marching her away, like a prisoner.

The next day I went back to look after the girls and Mrs. Rossiter actually arranged for me to talk to Ronnie. "He won't listen to me, Beatrice," she said. "His father has telephoned from London and talked to him but he is set on joining up. I believe he's in the garden." She looked at me and I couldn't believe it – the upright, self-confident woman had gone and her eyes were full of tears. "Please talk to him," she said.

I found Ronnie slumped on a stone bench by the rose garden. I shall always remember the scent of the big, overblown roses. He smiled at me as I sat beside him, conscious that his mother was standing on the terrace, looking down at us.

A light breeze blew rose petals over us, like a newly

wedded couple. If only – but I knew with a terrible foreboding that Ronnie would enlist whatever I said and that he would be killed.

"Elizabeth sent the white feather," I said. "She's really sorry."

"She wanted to avenge her brother's death," Ronnie said. He reached out for my hand and I moved closer to him. "I have seen such dreadful sights at the hospital. I want to help the wounded on the battlefield. There's a great need for stretcher-bearers and ambulance drivers. I've driven Mama's car round the lanes."

"Please stay. I can't bear it if you go." I began to cry.

"Beatrix – I have to prove I have courage. That I'm not just a feeble artist who hides behind a canvas."

"I love you." The words poured out before I could think.

"And I love you." He drew me closer. We were partly shielded by the roses but I could just see the white gleam of Mrs. R's nurses' hat.

Gently, he brushed the tears off my face and then he kissed me.

I heard Mrs. Rossiter calling me and we spun apart. I stood up and saw my brother Jimmy waving something at Mrs. Rossiter's face.

I clutched at Ronnie. "It might be news of Tod." Ronnie followed me as I hurried back to the terrace. I'd heard some soldiers went to the front line after only a few weeks' training. Supposing he had been wounded?"

"Mother told me not to come but I snatched the letter and ran all the way," Jimmy panted. "I knew you'd want to read it quick."

Mrs. Rossiter must have seen my expression. "Don't worry. It's not bad news," she said.

I read the letter: It was headed, "Training Camp – somewhere."

Dear Mother, Father and all of you.

As you can see, Tod and I are busy training and they didn't question our ages. It's boring stuff, marching about, learning about guns and suchlike and I can't wait to get out there. Tod has put in for working with the horses. We're both well but miss home cooking. Sorry to go off so suddenly but I had it in mind before the white feather came.

With love and good wishes, Alex. Tod sends his regards.

"So they aren't sending them back," Jimmy said proudly. "He's going to kill the Huns."

"Be quiet." I felt like slapping him.

Mrs. Rossiter brought out an immaculate white hand-kerchief and wiped her eyes. "I'm so sorry..." she said

"My brother is a good liar," I said then felt so disloyal. "Besides, he and Tod are six feet tall at least. I guess it wasn't hard to look eighteen."

Ronnie went away to London for several days – I imagined to see his father and the art school and I felt desolate because it felt as if he were already gone. His mother had arranged a concert at the hospital and she asked me to sing and Father to play the piano, moved from the main part of the Manor.

I had no heart for it but had to agree. Jem and the nurses helped the injured men to sit propped up in their beds or on chairs placed in the middle of the huge room, once a ballroom, I was told.

Elizabeth was playing the piano, singing a song from a Gilbert and Sullivan opera, something suitably sad about a wandering minstrel and a nightingale. I found it hard to go on forgiving her.

Father played for me and I sang *"Burlington Bertie"* again and at Mrs. Rossiter's suggestion *"Keep the Home Fires Burning,"* and *"Pack up your Troubles in your Old Kit Bag."* Some of the soldiers joined in.

It was warm and the crowded room smelled of Jeyes fluid, covering up a faint taint of rotting flesh. A dizzy faintness overcame me as I finished the songs. I tried to smile but almost staggered out to sit outside on the Veranda. I saw our pony look at me as he rested under a shady tree, harnessed to the Governess Cart.

The heat wave had come back and the wrought-iron seat was too hot, so I got up to sit on the browning grass. Then my head spun and I pitched into blackness.

"Put your head between your knees," Ronnie was saying and his arm was round me. I felt ridiculous but my head cleared and then I was in his arms, in full view of the main wing of the Manor.

"I'd just come back from London. As soon as I came into the room I saw you, pale as a white dove. Are you all right, Beatrix darling?" he asked.

"Darling." Nobody had ever called me that before.

"Yes," I whispered. "It was…the heat…"

"And the sight of those poor men." He stroked my hair and a shiver went through me, just as I imagined an electric current might feel. "I have something for you. Open it when you get home. I have to help the men back to bed at the end of the concert."

He handed me a small package, roughly wrapped in a piece of drawing paper and tied with string. He had painted two red hearts entwined, on a plain label.

Then Mrs. Rossiter was there and my parents, anxious abut me and Mother insisted on driving me home. I kept the parcel hidden in the folds of my skirt and when we arrived home, hurried to my room, saying I needed to rest.

My fingers trembled as I opened the little parcel and found a box. On top, Ronnie had written, "Will you marry me one day?" and inside was a plain silver ring. As I turned it in my fingers I saw there were tiny words inscribed inside: "*Always, your loving R.*" and the date.

My heart thudded and I nearly fainted again. Ronnie must have bought it when he went to London and had it inscribed – just for me. I couldn't believe it. I wanted to rush straight over to thank him and say "yes, yes – of course I'll marry you!" but I would have to wait until tomorrow.

I wondered if I had ever been as happy before.

Of course I couldn't wear the ring – Father would never let me become engaged at fifteen but I threaded it on a thin cord from my workbox and hung it round my neck, so the ring was concealed under my blouse.

I cycled at speed back to Tanglemere the next day, singing at the top of my voice. I passed a wagon laden with bales of straw from the harvest. This meant good luck – and that meant Ronnie wouldn't enlist and we could go on meeting.

It was like the first time I met them – the girls ran out of the house in their shifts and with bare feet but now they were crying. "Miss Denning – he's gone!" Herme shrieked.

Perse flung her arms round me. "Ronnie's gone to fight and Seli's crying."

At that moment Dante came running up to me, carrying a bloody white bundle. He dropped it at my feet, wagging his tail.

The girls screamed as they saw one of their doves, lying dead.

The blood was oozing from a wound in its white breast.

CHAPTER 12

I wanted to run home and hide in my room but I made myself go inside and comfort Mrs. Rossiter, who was standing in the hall, holding on to the carved bannister and crying silently. Without thinking that she might object, I ran and hugged her, pressing my face into her starched nurse's apron. The girls followed me and their mother held them with one arm, the other round me. Just for a moment, we were a family, mourning a lost son and I think Ronnie's mother guessed how much I loved him.

Then Mrs. Rossiter said she had to go to the hospital.

"There's a dead dove," Perse sobbed.

"I think there is more to worry about than a dead bird," her mother said but she smiled kindly.

I had to rid myself of the horror of the dead dove and the memory of the dove in my lap in the painting, the dove of peace who became a dove of war. I had to be brave for the girls' sake.

"Could we have a funeral?" Herme asked.

I knew I had to distract them, whatever I was feeling myself. "Of course. And we will sing a hymn too."

"And make a cross," Perse said.

"And put lots of flowers on," Herme said.

Maggs dug the hole by the tree house, muttering angrily about the dog taking one of 'his' doves. I saw the sharp puncture mark of the wound in the dove's white breast. Dante was a gun-dog, not likely to kill a bird and Mrs. Rossiter did not keep a cat. I wondered if a crow had killed it and imagined an aerial combat, the crow's dark wings overshadowing the terrified dove and the cruel beak thrusting at it. Alex had talked of the men who now flew airplanes to fight the war. "Just imagine – they fight in the air, lucky devils!"

This made me wonder what Alex and Tod were doing in the Army and then, of course I thought of Ronnie.

My face was wet with tears as the dove, wrapped by Perse in what looked like one of her mother's best tray-cloths, was lowered into the hole, covered with earth and then with flowers. The girls asked me to sing a hymn – as they never went to church they didn't know any religious songs – so I sang one verse of *"All things Bright and Beautiful, All Things Great and Small, All Things Wise and Wonderful, The Lord God Made them All*. When I got to the second verse and *"Each Little Bird That Sings,"* the girls began to cry. "I hate that God," Perse said. "Why didn't He look after our dove?"

I didn't answer her.

I cycled home that day aching all over with sadness, like an illness, and all the forgiveness I'd felt for Elizabeth melted away. I wanted to kill her because Ronnie had gone to war.

I had to do something. I cycled up the drive and pulled the bell outside the Manor door until it nearly fell off its chain. I must have looked pale and angry because the ancient butler moved back a step as he said, "Miss Elizabeth is out riding by the lake."

It was about two miles from the Manor and I was tired but I battled against a rising wind, which threw dust and twigs into my face. As I cycled along the narrow stony track, I remembered the last time when Ronnie and I sat on the carved log seat and kissed. How I hated Elizabeth!

My head was down, pushing against the wind and, too late, I saw the horse trotting towards me. It reared up and Elizabeth fell off with a scream. Then she lay still.

Had I wished her dead? I threw my cycle down and rushed

to her. I bent over her and saw she must have hit her head on a stone. Her eyes were shut and her mouth open. I felt a pulse in her neck and then she gave a faint moan. Should I lift her up? But supposing she'd broken something? I hoped she could hear me saying I'd fetch help.

The evil voice in my head said "she deserved it" but I tried not to listen. The chestnut horse was peacefully grazing and I caught the reins. If I could mount it, I'd get back quicker than on my bicycle.

It was an effort to heave myself up and I spoke to the horse all the while. It was hard to ride astride on a side-saddle but I managed somehow and as I jolted up and down I thought how stupid I'd been. Mother always said I was too impulsive. I was no rider and If I fell off, I'd be no help to Elizabeth.

The horse shied once when the wind blew leaves in its face but I managed to cling on to his mane. He trotted into the stable yard at the Manor and a stable-boy came running, and grabbed the reins. "Quiet, Brandy, quiet!" he soothed the horse. "Where's Miss Elizabeth?"

Elizabeth had bruises and concussion and she was kept in bed for a week. I forced myself to cycle through a storm to see her.

"Bea – you're soaked through," she said when I came up to her room. She tossed restlessly on her bed. "I don't remember what happened. They said you fetched help. Why were you there?" she asked.

I was tempted to lie. It would be easy to say I was taking her a message. I thought of my truthful parents and took a deep breath:

"I was angry with you because of Ronnie enlisting. I suppose I was going to slap your face." I looked at her pale face and stringy, unwashed hair and felt ashamed.

She gave a feeble smile. "I think I've had my slap on the face, don't you?" Her restless fingers pulled at the linen sheet.

"I'm really sorry. I pray every night that those three boys will be sent back." She sat up, with an effort, leaning forward to catch hold of my hand. "Bea – I have a real pain when I think of them and I can't believe I'll not see my brother again."

I found myself sitting on the bed, my arm round her, both of us crying.

When I got home, I was one moment shivering with cold and another hot with fever. Mother forced me to go to bed where I tossed and turned for days. Mother said Jem had called with fresh eggs, asking after me but she didn't want to come in and catch the fever as she was still working at the hospital. She also told Mother that they now had one of the new Land Girls working on the farm now Tod was gone.

Each day, I asked if Alex had written or if there was a letter for me. I couldn't believe Ronnie would give me the ring and then lose touch completely. Was he at the Front? Supposing…no – I wouldn't go there. Mother tried to look cheerful but I knew she was hiding her worry.

Ronnie had been at a public school and Father told me those boys went straight to Flanders after very little training. It was thought that they were born to be officers.

"Class distinction, as usual," Father said. His face was carved into a disapproving mask and wild sounds of Chopin and Beethoven thundered up into my room.

August thunderstorms made me think this must be like gunfire. I tried to think of Alex, but after all, he wanted to be in the Army and I just knew he had a charmed life – he would survive and thrive on it.

Mrs. Rossiter came to see me, carrying a huge bunch of late summer flowers and painted home-made cards from the girls. "No word yet," she said. "But I expect they are far too occupied to write. Come back soon, Beatrice. The girls miss you and they are driving Mrs. Maggs mad!" Her laugh was forced.

I was up at last but still weak, reading my favourite book,

Little Women, where the girls waited for a father involved in yet another war, in America, when Mother gave me the letter from Ronnie. I felt faint for a moment as I opened the envelope. There was an Army address at the top.

My Beata Beatrix.

Forgive me for being too cowardly to say goodbye but I think of you every day, my beautiful girl. I am driving an ambulance behind the front line and helping with the wounded in the Field Hospital. I'm eighteen next week so they won't send me back. At first, the sights and sounds horrified me but I am so busy and so tired now that I feel numb. The reality is you, not the battle round me, and I try to imagine your lovely face and our life together in the future.

Please write to me, my dear love. Your Ronnie. xxx

I sat in my room composing a letter to him, tearing up several copies. In the end, I just said I would always love him and please come home safely.

Then I found a piece of water-colour paper and designed a birthday card for him. He might smile at the amateur effort, but I did my best to draw a dove enclosed in a red heart and decorated all round with red roses and leaves. Then I went out for the first time, taking the letter to our village Post Office where the white-haired Postmistress, Miss Hebbes, looked carefully at the address and then at me, until I blushed. "One of our brave boys," she murmured as she took the stamped and bulky letter.

Miss Hyacinth Hebbes was the village gossip so I hurried off before she could ask me any questions. I kept Ronnie's letter in my pocket and re-read it until it was thoroughly crumpled.

At last I cycled back to Tanglemere where the girls rushed out to hug me and welcomed me back. How could I ever have thought them merely little savages?.

"At least he has written," Mrs. Rossiter said when I arrived. She adjusted her high collar and composed her face. "We must be brave, Beatrice."

I felt a tiny bit better, that she had accepted that Ronnie and I loved one another and now she called me 'Beatrice' and not the formal 'Miss Denning'. When I had a moment to spare from the girls, I went to the studio and looked at his paintings, and especially at my portrait. I wished he hadn't put the dead dove in my lap.

I hardly saw Jem, who was working at the hospital whenever she could be spared from the farm.

When Jimmy came back from school he was unusually quiet. "Will Alex get killed?" he asked. I tried to reassure him but it helped next day when Alex's letter arrived. Mother read it out for Father and we sat at the breakfast table, listening to every word.

"Chere Mamon et Papa, La Tadpole and Jimmy,

I am sorry I haven't written before but the training took up a great deal of time and now I am in a VERY MUDDY trench in Flanders. The other fellows are a good bunch. Tod is in the same Regiment but looking after the horses, which is right up his street. We look proper soldiers now we have uniforms, rifles and bayonets. We look like grotesque frogs in our gas-masks!

I am thin but fit, eating whatever is given (not enough!) The water has been chlorinated and tastes terrible. I think about Mother's home-made lemonade or the beer which I might have drunk, if it hadn't exploded in the cellar last year!

The gunfire reminds me of Bonfire Night. It's hard to sleep but I am getting used to it and am trying to make friends with the rats and lice (joke!)

Dear Ma and Father – I am sorry for going off like that but I wanted to be a soldier. I don't think I'm cut out for university…

Tell Jimmy to behave himself and Taddy – I promise I won't tease you any more when I'm home on leave.

Parcels seem to get here – please send wool socks and a big jumper – it will get cold at night soon. Also Oxo cubes, tins of bully beef and chocolate would be acceptable.

My love to you all, Alex.

Then Jem came round with a letter from Tod.

"I'm with the horses and some of them hate the gunfire – others get wounded and have to be shot. They burn the bodies and it's a terrible stink. I miss the farm and you all and hope it'll all be over soon. Meantime, maybe I can help by looking after the poor horses. Why should they be maimed and killed in our war?

I try to remember the happy times – skating on the Mere – Bea riding my Star – except that makes me sad. I keep hoping I might see Star out here but pigs might fly!

I hope you are all well. Love from Tod."

"He's still thinking of you," Jem's eyes were hard.

I felt terrible. I was fond of Tod and hate to think he was so unhappy. "Shall I write to him?" I asked.

"Better not. I have to go now."

I felt really bad as my best pal cycled away, still angry with me.

CHAPTER 13

I couldn't believe it – Ronnie was on his way home! Mrs. Rossiter's usually dignified face was charged with excitement when she told me. "His ambulance was hit by gunfire and overturned – he's broken his arm. He spent a week at a hospital on the coast but the bone will take time to heal, so they're sending him home to our little hospital."

I felt like dancing and singing! The black feeling of ill-omen I'd felt when I saw the dead dove had been wrong. Ronnie was injured but safe. "Does it mean he won't have to go back?" I asked.

Mrs. Rossiter was getting ready for the hospital, trying to do up her high white collar. "This ridiculous thing!" She tugged at it angrily. "Beatrice – I think if his arm heals well, he will have to go back. He's eighteen now, the age for enlisting."

I wanted to meet the train but I was told nurses would escort the soldiers into the new ambulance, paid for by Lady Drummond. Now Sally, the Land Girl, was at the farm, Jem spent more time at the hospital and she would be there, helping the injured men. "You needn't come," she snapped but I found the time from her and went to the station.

The men shuffled oute of the station, some on crutches, some bandaged and all of them with bedraggled, dirty uniform and completely expressionless faces.

"He's not there, Jem," I wanted to cry.

"He is. Last one," she said and ran to help the men into the ambulance.

I hardly recognised him. He shuffled along with his arm in a dirty sling like an old man, his head low. I waved and even called out, getting curious looks from the small crowd of villagers.

At last, just as Jem was helping him into the ambulance, he looked up and saw me. He raised his good arm in a kind of stiff salute. His face was dead white and I felt a shiver of alarm.

When I told Mother I was going to see him at the Manor hospital, she looked worried: "Remember, Bea dear – he's been wounded and seen dreadful sights. He may be very different."

I had tried not to talk about Ronnie at home because we had no more news of Alex and I knew my parents were anxious and sad. I wondered, if I could, would I swap Ronnie's safe return for Alex's? I realised the dreadful truth, I wouldn't. Ronnie was home and that filled my entire being.

Mrs. Rossiter had given me time off from my duties to see Ronnie but she warned me visiting hours were short and the Matron very fierce. I had hoped she might meet me at the hospital but she said she was too busy and I daren't ask Jem.

I first looked in on what was once the Manor ballroom – where I'd entertained the soldiers on that hot day which now felt ages ago. I'd never forget that day because it was the last time I'd seen Ronnie, when he gave me the ring.

A nurse saw me. "The newly-arrived wounded go to Ward 2," she said and directed me to what I remembered was the Long Gallery in the Manor, which was lined with portraits of Elizabeth's ancestors.

I waited outside the ward with an old couple and a girl who said she had travelled all day to see her fiance. At last we were allowed inside.

The smell hit me – a mixture of disinfectant and the stink of running sores, blood and worse – just as Jem had said. How could she bear working here?

There were beds only on one side of this ward and I walked slowly down, feeling sick with apprehension. Ronnie's mother said he would be changed – supposing he didn't love me any more?

Men were groaning and one was calling out for his mother in a weak voice. I passed a bed where a boy younger than Alex called out to me, gurgled words I couldn't make out. I felt sick when I saw his jaw was so damaged it was supported by a bandage. And what had happened to his arms?

I looked for Mrs Rossiter but she wasn't there – she often helped in the operating theatre, I'd heard. Jem was busy scrubbing an empty iron bed frame, her hands red and sore-looking from hot water and Jeyes Fluid. I spoke to her and she answered briefly. "I don't suppose you'll care too much but Tod has been wounded. He's being taken to a hospital at Dover."

"Of course I care," I said. "Is he bad?"

"Might lose his foot," she snapped. "Your precious Ronnie is in the end bed."

"Miss Mason is here to work, not talk." Matron rustled up to me. She had the makings of a black moustache and scary black eyebrows.

I escaped from her and hurried down the ward.

Ronnie was propped up, his arm in a clean sling now. His eyes were dull in a dead white face and at first he hardly reacted when I said, stupidly, "I'm here – Ronnie, it's your Beatrice."

"Beatrice." He stared at me, then smiled at last. "Thank you for coming."

"Of course I had to come. Is the pain bad?" I sat on a hard stool by his bed and gingerly touched his good left arm. He was left-handed so his painting hand was safe.

"Not too bad,." he muttered. "But it's the nightmares I get."

"Was it awful out there?"

"Worse than I could tell you. I wish I hadn't to go back."

"But you can't – I mean, your arm…"

"It's actually the top of my shoulder and upper arm. The wound was infected in the Field Hospital – they'd run out of everything, disinfectant, bandages the lot – men were dying like flies. So that's why they sent me home. But as soon as it heals, I shall have a medical check and get sent back, I know."

There was a clatter as one of the nurses dropped something. Ronnie clutched my hand and I could feel the deep shivers going through him. "Sorry. I can't bear sudden noises. Reminds me of the gunfire. It went on and on and on…" Suddenly tears fell down his face and he looked away. "Perhaps I'm not brave enough," he said in a muffled voice. "Some men have been over there for months. It got to me within weeks and I was almost glad to be wounded."

I hated seeing him cry. Jimmy cried when he fell out of a tree or fought with his friends but I had never seen a man cry.

"I won't let you go back." I made a resolve, there and then.

"They need ambulance drivers and stretcher-bearers. I was useful."

"Please…" I began but a bell was being rung vigorously and a nurse called out, "Visiting time is over. Please leave the ward."

I wanted to ask him if he still loved me but I couldn't. I just kissed his good hand and walked out, crying.

Mrs. Rossiter came into the hall just as I was leaving. "Don't cry," she said, putting her hand on my shoulder. "He's getting better.

"But he says he'll be sent back. He's all sort of shaky…"

"Some shell-shock, certainly. But he is still in the Army. His father is coming to see him. Perhaps he can pull strings – he has painted portraits of the wives of several Generals."

Pulling strings, as if Ronnie were a puppet but perhaps that's what he was, with all the other soldiers, puppets directed by stupid Generals who probably were safely behind the lines or even in England.

CHAPTER 14

I went every day to the Manor Hospital and held Ronnie's hand, talking of the happy times we'd had together, reminding him of the portrait, trying to remove that shocked, dull expression from his face.

One day, I found Elizabeth waiting outside the ward. "What are you here for?" I asked rudely.

"I have to tell him I'm sorry." She looked pale, almost ghostly, in her black dress and I wondered spitefully if she minded leaving off her bright, expensive clothes to go into mourning for Edwin.

"If you want," I said ungraciously.

"At least he won't have to go back."

"He's pretty certain he will."

"He's under age."

"Not in October."

"Can't he hide or something?" She must have looked desperate because the small group of visitors waiting stared at her.

I'd said something like that to Ronnie but he'd answered that the Military Police, the Redcaps, searched for AWOL – Absent without Leave – soldiers. I lowered my voice. "They'd find him in our small village quite quickly."

"London," she said. "He could dye his hair or something. He's an art student. He must know places to stay."

At that moment the doors opened and Jem came out, carrying a covered bed-pan. She stopped suddenly when she saw Elizabeth. "Damn you to Hell!" she said and – I don't know if it was deliberate or not – some of the stinking contents slopped onto Elizabeth's ankles and shiny shoes.

"Jem…" I began, seeing the waiting visitors draw back but she swept along the corridor as if nothing had happened.

Ronnie was up, sitting on a hard chair by the bed. He looked surprised when he saw Elizabeth, who put a basket of grapes and hot-house peaches on the bed-table.

She was crimson-faced and I could smell the stink from her ankles and feet. "I'll never forgive myself for sending that white feather." Her voice was high with tension. "It was awful of me. I was out of my mind over Edwin's death."

Ronnie smiled, that gorgeous big smile I knew so well. "I guess I'd have to go some time anyway. You must miss Edwin so much."

Tears fell down her face. "I do." Then she lowered her voice. "Don't go back. You could hide in our stables. The horrible Army people have taken all our horses now, even my darling Brandy. He hates sudden noises – he'll bolt if a gun goes off."

Ronnie put out his good hand and touched her arm. "I know. This war's not fair on the horses. Thank you for the offer but your mother might object."

"She's fallen apart since Edwin died. Her favourite, you know. My father thinks he died gallantly and in a good cause. Papa's a stupid old soldier who loves war." Suddenly she saw Jem coming back, and hurried away.

"Poor Elizabeth," Ronnie said and I had to agree with him.

Jem came up and refilled Ronnie's water-jug. "Got rid of that girl!" she muttered. She looked down at Ronnie. "You're doing better than my poor brother."

"Are you going to see him?"

"Tomorrow. It's a long train journey to Dover. Just my mum and me. We can't leave the land-girl on her own at the farm."

I wanted to ask her if I could come with them. My heart was with Ronnie but I had to see Tod, my pal from way back. Now

I was in love myself, I realised how much he must be hurting, not just physically – but because he loved me.

Before I could speak, the nurse called Jem away.

Ronnie looked at me. "You need to see him, Bea." He must have read my mind. "I can give you money for the journey. I may be going home tomorrow so I won't lack for company with those sisters of mine pestering me."

I saw his mother striding through the ward, coming to see him and I knew she would want me to get back to the girls before Mrs. Maggs gave notice.

Perse and Herme were making a banner for Ronnie – already they had stuck pieces of paper together and had written in huge untidy capitals, WELLCUM HOME RONNIE. I hadn't the heart to correct the spelling.

They were now decorating it with pictures, of flowers, birds and little stick-figures representing themselves, their mother and – I was rather touched when Perse pointed to a hugely tall figure with a smiley face and lots of bright ginger hair – "That's you, Miss Denning," she said.

When Mrs. Rossiter came home, I asked if I could take the day off to visit Jem's brother in Dover. She gave me a strange look but pressed a guinea into my hand for the train journey.

"All that way, on your own, Bea!" Mother looked surprised and rather hurt. "I thought as we've no news from Alex you would be with us more – but you've been visiting Ronnie Rossiter each day. Jimmy's upset, not hearing from Alex and he's always getting into fights in the village after school. And as for your father..." She paused. Loud piano music was coming from the parlour. "He gets me to read the newspaper to him and accounts of the war upsets him, especially as he says the real facts are hidden. But now they are publishing lists of casualties. They are so long." She sighed. "I had to persuade him to go on playing the organ in church because he says the Vicar is anti-Christian, spreading hatred of the Germans and making out our soldiers are dying in a good cause. And I am thinking of Cousin Frederick. I wonder if he has had to leave his lecturing post at the University and join the Army?"

Of course I felt guilty. Mother, never fat, had lost weight so her clothes hung about her and meals were fractured with Father telling Jimmy off, sending him to bed, quite often in tears.

She stopped kneading the bread-dough and looked at me. "Speaking of Cousin Frederick – have you told anyone you have German relations?"

"Only Jem – I showed her one of his lovely Christmas cards one year. And of course Miss Hebbes at the Post Office – when she saw the German stamp."

"Someone threw eggs at the window when you were out. And last week, you remember there was a broken pane of glass in the scullery window? I let you think it was Jimmy, throwing a hard ball. I'll show you." She wiped her floury hands and fetched a tattered piece of paper on which was written, GET OUT BLUDDY HUNS. "That was wrapped round the stone. I haven't told your father and of course he can't see the hole in the window."

"Did you tell Constable Goodchild?"

"I did – but I didn't show him the message. He blames one of the gypsy boys who came to help with harvesting at the Mason's farm but I think it's village lads. The gypsies wouldn't have heard of our relations."

Everyone always put all thieving and trouble on the big Smith family of gypsies, who arrived each year on the Common. It was an easy way out, I thought. I wondered about Jem. She'd never...

"Don't worry, Bea. I believe this has happened to other people. And whoever wrote it isn't well educated. The Constable recommended getting a dog – and I am thinking about it."

"Floss won't like it!" I tried to laugh, to make light of the whole thing, but I knew Mother was upset. The evil of war seemed to give birth to more and more hate.

That night I was a long time going to sleep and then I dreamed that a white dove perched on my arm and cooed to me as I went through a field, red with poppies – then the sky was filled with huge black wings as crows dived down and carried off my dove, blood dripping down from the sky like a red sunset. I woke up muttering, "A murder of crows..."

CHAPTER 15

I was squashed between a soldier and a fat woman who never stopped eating buns, washed down by tea from a Thermos jug. This was my second train in one day.

I had only been on the local train to the High School but this journey involved changing trains twice, the second time in London, a city new to me. I'd found out the times of the trains from the ancient clerk at the station. With Jem in her present mood, it might be better not to travel with the Masons, so I stayed in the stuffy waiting-room until I saw them arrive on the platform.

When the train steamed into the station, I let them get on before I jumped into the last carriage, a Ladies Only. It was a warm day but the window was shut and when I let the leather strap out to lower it, an old lady said we'd be covered with soot from the engine. The rest of the compartment was packed with Canaries, as we called them, girls with hair and skin dyed yellow from the gunpowder in the armaments factory where they worked. They were chattering just like their namesakes and didn't seem to notice the heat.

Grammar School and High School boys and girls got off with the factory girls at the town and I thought if it wasn't for the war, Alex might still be going to school. I could hardly believe I was the same person, who used to travel with Jem on this very train to school. Jem, with her ambitions to become a doctor while I had to earn money and try to find a way of getting into the theatre.

Only months back, I was still a schoolchild, giggling with Jem like the Canaries. Now I was almost a woman, sixteen in October, and I was in love for the first time and I was sure, for the last time.

Changing trains in the huge London station was alarming but it was easy to avoid the Masons in that great throng of people pressed round me.

This train was packed and I couldn't get into the Ladies Only carriage and had to squash into a carriage packed with people and soldiers.

The war seemed far away as we steamed through placid countryside, where the little tents of straw stooks marched like soldiers across the harvested fields. I thought of Ronnie and tried to work out how I could stop him going back. It was hard to concentrate as the soldier next to me fell asleep and to my horror, his cap fell off and his head was slid onto my shoulder. He smelled of sweat and unwashed clothes and there were fleas crawling in his greasy hair.

I tried to move away but the fat woman dug her elbow into me and her four soot-spotted children giggled from the opposite seat, swinging their booted feet so I was regularly kicked.

At last the train steamed into the station and I got out, pushing my way through the crowds. This time, I saw Mrs. Mason's best hat decorated with artificial poppies bobbing amongst the crowds. I'd planned to ask my way to the hospital but it would be easier to follow them.

The Masons got into one of the horse-drawn cabs outside the station and I took the next one, feeling reckless at the expense. I had brought some of my earnings but I was glad of Mrs. Rossiter's guinea. I asked the cab-driver to follow the Masons' cab to the hospital.

He leered at me. "Visiting your sweetheart, love?"

I took no notice. Soon I had my first sight of the blue sea between the buildings and I wished it was a happier occasion.

If only I could be running along the sands with Ronnie, healed and out of the Army's cruel grasp.

Again I saw Mrs. Mason's hat bobbing ahead and Jem, tall beside her so I followed them at a distance, down dreary green-painted corridors until they stopped to ask a nurse the way. I let them get ahead and then followed them through green doors into a huge ward.

The smell was rather worse than in the Manor Hospital and I tried not to look at the wounded men, some groaning and others asleep.

The Masons went to the end of the ward and through curtains, pulled round a bed. My heart beat so fast I almost choked. Did the curtains mean Tod was very ill…dying? And how was I going to see him without meeting the Masons? Mother always did say I plunged into things without thinking ahead and I suppose she was right.

Then I saw a nurse come out with a cloth over a basin or chamber-pot and I guessed that was why the curtains were drawn.

I hung back, feel stupid and wondering why I had come. The Masons would certainly not want to see me and I was afraid Tod would think me fonder of him than I was.

Suddenly Jem came through the curtains, supporting her mother.

I could see Mrs. Mason's face was paper-white and her eyes were closed. She must be in some kind of faint and a nurse ran forward to help Jem. "She needs fresh air," Jem was saying and then she saw me. "Bea! Why are you here?" Her voice was cold.

"I wanted to see him. Let me help you," I said. "Is your mother ill?"

"The sight of his foot and leg made her feel faint. I'm used to it."

The nurse went to find a chair and we almost carried Mrs. Mason to the corridor, where there was an open window.

"She'll be all right. You go and see him," Jem said. "He asked after you. I said you were fussing round Ronnie at the Manor hospital. I didn't want to give him any hopes."

I left them and approached Tod's bed feeling like crying. The curtains were drawn back now and I saw there was some kind of support over his legs. His face was flushed and at first I thought he couldn't be so ill.

"Bea – is that really you?" he said hoarsely. Sweat was trickling down his face.

"It's really me!" I tried to smile and went to hold his hand. It was damp and hot. "Have you got a fever? How did you get wounded?"

"I was in charge of the horses. Poor devils, some starving, some blown to bits but mine survived. Then they took fright and pulled the gun-carriage wheel over my foot. It's infected, gangrene they call it. May have to come off."

I didn't know what to say. "That's awful." Did he expect me to look at his foot as the Masons had done?

He pulled on my hand so I was near from his face. His breath stank of illness but I didn't move. "They don't know. Don't tell. It wasn't an accident." He stopped.

I was confused. "What do you mean?"

He went on in a low voice. "I put my foot under the wheel."

I didn't know what to say.

"Don't think less of me for it," he said in a pleading voice. "I wasn't out there very long but it was like Hell. Mud, wounded men, terrible noise from the shelling but the worst was the horses' suffering. I kept thinking of Star, going through all that. We was being shelled to bits – our Company was retreating when I saw the Captain's horse – a beauty, very like Star - bolting back, jumping over shell-holes, taking him to safety. Then it fell, breaking a leg. They shot it. The bloody Army doesn't care for men nor beast. They shoot German prisoners, they shoot poor young sods who get lost and run the wrong way. I couldn't stand it any more." He fell back, looking exhausted.

I thought of Ronnie and how he didn't want to go back. "I understand," I said. "It must have been so terrible."

"Some men put their hands up over the trenches so they'd get shot. But the Army was wise to that. They believed me, though." His hand clutched mine like a life-line.

"You'll get better." The words seemed feeble. How would I know? "Perhaps they'll bring you to the Manor. Ronnie Rossiter's there. He was injured when his ambulance turned over."

He let go my hand. "Sorry to hear about it. And no – I'll not be at the Manor Hospital. Didn't you know it was for officers and NCOs, not us lot?" He stopped. "Bea, what's that round your neck?"

To my horror, I found the chain and ring had somehow escaped my blouse, partly unbuttoned because of the heat, and it was swinging right in front of Ronnie's eyes.

"It's – a keepsake…" I stammered.

"It's a ring. From Ronnie Rossiter?"

"Yes."

"You got him back, anyway."

I couldn't bear it – my dearest friend Tod had tears in his eyes.

"Yes, but he's almost well. He will have to go back when he passes his medical examination – but he doesn't want to. I think he's a bit shell-shocked."

Tod struggled to sit up and I went to help him and gave him a drink from the glass of water by the bed. "Tell him, tell him to hide. Don't let him go back." He was breathing fast. "I love you enough Bea, to wish you happiness with him. Help him."

Then he slumped, his eyes closed.

Jem ran to the bed. "You've upset him!" Her voice was angry.

He half-opened his eyes. "I wanted to see her, Jem. Don't be angry…" Then he slept again.

CHAPTER 16

Perhaps Tod's words made Jem relent because her mother asked me to share a cab with them and I travelled all the way home with them in the train. We were all exhausted by the journey and even more by our sadness and shock at seeing Tod, who had left home for the Army strong and healthy and now might be crippled for life.

"At least he'll be coming home for good," was all Mrs. Mason said. She'd recovered her usual high colour but her eyelids were swollen from crying.

I wouldn't wish Ronnie to be crippled too but I envied the Masons, knowing their Tod would never go back to the Army.

It was almost dark when we got back and as we trudged off our separate ways from the station, Jem said, "Sorry I was so angry. At least you made the effort to see him."

I felt just a little happier as I walked home down the dark street.

Growls and barks greeted me as I opened the front door and I was almost knocked over by a large dog.

Jimmy came running. "Down, Bertie!" he said. "Jem – we got a dog now to keep the baddies away." He hugged the wolf-like dog who was wagging his tail as well as growling at me.

Hearing the commotion, Father came into the hall. "You're safely back, Beatrice." He edged forward, putting his hand out to the dog, who licked it. "The Constable found this Alsation for us – before the war the breed was called a German Shepherd but of course, the name had to be changed because people can't stand anything German. He's only young but Jimmy has promised to train him – and perhaps he might lead me about. Before the war, your mother read me a newspaper article about a man – I think a German, strangely enough – who trained a dog to lead a blind man about."

"That would be wonderful." But I could only think of Ronnie.

"By the time Alex comes back I'll have Bertie trained up to take you out, Father," Jimmy said happily.

I heard a faint sigh from Mother and I knew what she was thinking. Why hadn't we heard from Alex?

"How did Floss react to a dog?" I was hoping to divert her thoughts from worries about my brother.

She smiled. "She spat at him and he was so scared he hid behind a chair."

I was glad they had a dog to protect them because now I felt sure I had to leave home soon, to hide Ronnie away in London.

When I went back to Tanglemere the next day, I had a surprise.

"He's home!" Perse and Herme rushed at me as soon as I got in.

The WELCUM HOME notice was drooping from the carved banisters in the hall.

I found Ronnie sitting at the kitchen table, eating a slice of Mrs.Maggs' best fruit cake while she was trimming round a pie-crust. His sling was gone and his eyes were brighter.

"Bea!" He smiled and stood up. I knew he would have embraced me if Mrs. Maggs hadn't been there. "I missed you yesterday. See – my shoulder is nearly better and I can move my hand."

I wasn't sure this was good news. "But of course you're not well enough to go back," I said.

"That's what I say," Mrs. Maggs joined in rather breathlessly, as she bent with difficulty to put the finished pie in the oven.

"I have a medical examination at the end of the week." He sat down again and I noticed his hand shaking as he picked up his cup of tea. "My mama told me you went to see Tod. How is he?"

"Not good. He may lose his foot."

"Poor chap! That makes my troubles very small."

The girls burst into the kitchen and Perse picked up a lump of uncooked pastry, stuffing it into her mouth. "You take those girls out of my kitchen!" Mrs. Maggs bellowed. "In this house nobody's remembered that old motto, 'Spare the rod and spoil the child' A good spanking is what those young ladies need sometimes."

I took them away.

It was very hard, keeping them busy and knowing Ronnie was in the house or garden and we couldn't really talk. Mrs. Rossiter came back before I went and asked me to come into the drawing-room where Ronnie was now sitting, a book in his lap..

"Matron told me off for leaving early." She smiled "But as I'm a volunteer she can't say too much. Don't you think Ronnie looks much better, Beatrice?" She looked fondly at him.

He smiled at me. "My arm is mending up only too well."

"Yes, but…" I began

She knew at once what I was thinking. "If he passes the medical – my husband suggests he goes to stay with him or at least goes to London where the military might not find him." She frowned. "But I don't know that Ronnie would go and anyway, there is another person living in the house already."

She obviously didn't want to talk about Mr. Rossiter's actress friend.

"The Redcaps – the Military Police – would easily find me there," Ronnie's voice was low and depressed. "And now I'm eighteen, I can't plead my age." He was reaching for a glass of water on the table when suddenly there was a crash and a yell from upstairs, where the girls were supposed to be tidying their room. His hand shook so much that he knocked the glass over.

"My stupid nerves," he said, trying to smile.

"That's shell-shock," his mother said. "You shouldn't go back."

"That's up to the Army. I've seen men come back from hospital who still shake and can't sleep. Anyway, wouldn't I be a coward, trying to hide?"

"No!" I found myself shouting – not caring that my employer was staring at me.

But she said, "Beatrice is right. I need to talk to you, Ronnie."

I saw him each day that week and we even sat on the garden seat again. The roses had died and autumn was coming. I wondered why he didn't sit closer or try to kiss me. I longed to hold him in my arms again.

"Do you still love me?" I asked the day before his Army medical.

He smiled at me but his eyes were sad. "Of course I do. Always. But if I have to return, I don't want you to miss me too much."

I knew he meant he might die. Father said so many were killed after just a few weeks on the front. "So they send more. Cannon-fodder!" he had raged.

"I won't let you go." I reached for his hand and he did kiss me then, but only lightly, on the cheek.

Mrs. Rossiter drove him to his Army Medical early one morning and I didn't see him until the afternoon. I set the girls to work on a play they were writing together and found him in the studio, looking at my portrait, now framed and propped against the wall.

"What happened?" My heart was banging so hard I thought he'd hear it.

He picked up the painting. "I want you to have this. They say I am well enough to rejoin the Battalion."

"When?"

"I have to report for duty right away. I need to pack."

I took the framed painting but put it down again and went to hug him. Perhaps I was shameless but I didn't care. "Please don't go." I whispered.

His arms were round me and then we were kissing and he drew me to the couch where I'd posed for him. He kissed my eyes, my nose and then lingered over my mouth and his breathing was coming fast.

I felt as if I was melting, that I'd do anything he wanted.

Then he stopped and drew back as he had before. "No, you're too young. It's not fair to you."

I was nearly in tears. "Always too young! I'm nearly sixteen. And it's not fair to me if you get killed."

The dogs were barking outside and we both sprang apart. I was buttoning up my blouse when Elizabeth came in.

"Mrs. Maggs told me where you were." She looked at Ronnie. "She said the Army are sending you back." Her voice rose, almost hysterically. "You can't go! If you are killed it will be all my fault."

Were those tears falling down her face genuine? I still didn't wholly trust her. And even now, she was talking of her feelings rather than Ronnie's and mine.

"You mustn't blame yourself, Elizabeth," he said.

"You have to hide." She came over and clutched at his arm.

"They'll find me. Soldiers who go AWOL – absent without leave – are prosecuted and end up in prison, like as not."

Her face was white and her anguish genuine. "Please, Bea, persuade him. Hide him at our stables till the Redcaps have gone and you can plan to get him to London. There's a mattress where our stable-boy used to sleep. I can bleach his hair blonde."

So her blonde hair wasn't totally natural after all. I was

ashamed that this trivia pleased me.

"It won't work," he said but I could sense he was weakening.

"You'll have friends still at the art school – they'll help find you somewhere to live."

I didn't want to point out that if those Redcaps were so vigilant they would probably go to the Slade to make enquiries.

Suddenly it didn't matter to me that it was Elizabeth who wanted to help, spiteful Elizabeth who had sent the white feathers. And it didn't matter so much that obviously she was still sweet on him and hoped to get some kind of advantage over me, by helping.

Nothing mattered but hiding Ronnie from the Military Police but here he was, his head in his hands, muttering "I don't want to be branded a coward!"

CHAPTER 17

I woke with a sick feeling in my stomach. Elizabeth and I had done our best to try persuading Ronnie to hide but he just said, "Leave me alone!" and rushed off to the studio. At least he wasn't packing – yet. When I left, Mrs. Rossiter had gone to talk to him but I didn't think she would succeed. Why did men have such pride? As she'd said, he wasn't fit to go back and lead men into danger.

Mother saw my white face at breakfast – I'd tossed and turned all night. I'd told both of them at supper about Ronnie's medical and Father had exploded into one of his rare rages:

"He's obviously got some shell-shock. It's terrible to send him back to fight. This war..." He'd rushed to his beloved piano and we heard his hands strike loud chords.

"You don't look well, darling. Would you like to stay at home today?" Mother said now. "I can send Jimmy with a message before school."

"I'm all right. I'd rather go to work." How could I tell her I had to hide Ronnie? That was, if he hadn't gone to his Army HQ already.

A black Staff car passed me as I cycled up the drive to Tanglemere and I had a brief glimpse of two men in Army uniform, wearing red caps. The car was gone before I could be quite sure there wasn't another man in the back.

The dogs rushed to greet me and the girls flew out of the front door in their night-shifts. "They've come for him!"

Herme said and Perse burst into tears.

They both clung to me. "Mrs. Maggs said she didn't know where he was but they said they'd come back. He's in the loft above the studio. We'll tell him those nasty men have gone."

The girls ran ahead of me and I found Ronnie brushing the cobwebs off himself and the loft door open above the studio. "Mama made me promise to hide before she went to work." He was smiling but his face was pale. "They've caught up with me so quickly. I might as well give myself up. I'm sure they'll be back."

"No!" I shouted and the girls clung round him. "Fetch that dressing-up box," I told them. "I'm going to disguise your brother and take him away. Hurry up now." They ran off.

He looked at me, almost angrily. "How?"

"I'll fetch our pony and cart and take you to hide in the Drummonds' stables. We can go round the back way, so we don't pass the Manor. When they've finished searching the village, you can get the train to London."

The girls heaved in the wicker box and I searched amongst the props and dresses already in the studio.

Twenty minutes later and after some arguing with him, he was changed.

Ronnie stared at himself in the long cheval mirror. "I look totally ridiculous!"

The girls were giggling but I told them to be quiet. He was wearing a worn black cloak over a long black skirt and his hair was hidden by a huge purple hat, decorated with black feathers. I'd found a feather boa to put round his only too masculine neck. There was no disguising his large male feet but I hoped nobody would look right into the Governess cart. "If anyone should ask, I shall say you are Mrs. Maggs' sister, applying for a position at the Manor."

"Supposing they come right back now?" He pulled irritably at the skirt. "I can't think how women walk in such hampering clothes."

"Now you know how lucky you men are!" I said. "Now you must hide again but don't get too cobwebby. I won't be long."

I told the girls to go back to the schoolroom and make their brother a card to wish him luck. They promised to keep it secret from Mrs. Maggs where he was going.

"I'll draw a black cat," Perse said.

"No! I thought of it first," said Herme and they went off arguing.

I had to pass the entrance to the Manor on my ride back and a car behind hooted so loudly I nearly fell off my bicycle.

The black Staff car rolled through the entrance to the Manor. They were already checking the hospital and perhaps even the Manor itself. Was there any point in hiding him in those stables?

CHAPTER 18

I still went ahead with the plan because I couldn't think of anything else although ideas of hiding Ronnie in the woods flitted through my mind but he would need shelter and food.

I hadn't any idea what to tell Mother but I found them both out and remembered Father talking of practice at the church for the organ recital he was giving in aid of the troops. It was a good thing the church was so near or they might have taken Tommy. Jimmy must be still at school.

I left Bertie barking indignantly in the house and fetched Tommy's harness before I lured him with an apple.

"Where are you going with him?"

I looked up and saw Jem.

Should I tell her? The fewer people knowing about Ronnie hiding the better.

"Why've you come?" I asked as Tommy bent his head obligingly for the collar.

"I wanted to ask how Ronnie was. Has he had his medical? I couldn't sleep last night for thinking about it and worrying about Tod."

I stared at her, surprised at her change of manner. It was so unlike Jem, who always seemed to be so strong, never apprehensive or fanciful like me.

She patted Tommy's head. "I'm still angry that Alex took Tod with him – but I suppose you can't help being sweet on Ronnie. And Tod's not going to be fit for courting anyone for a long while. So – what happened?"

I told her. "Then Elizabeth Drummond came along and said she'd hide him in their stables till he could get to London."

She stared at me. "You're quite daft! The Manor buildings will be the first place they'll search."

"I've just seen the Army car go through their gates. So maybe they won't come back. But I don't know what else to do."

Her strong hands were doing up the buckles of Tommy's harness. "You'd better bring Ronnie to the farm. The barn's big enough but of course, he can't stay long. I don't want Mum and Da to get into trouble, harbouring an AWOL soldier. Bea – you don't think things out, do you? How're you going to drive him through the village? Someone'll recognise him."

How typical of Jem to be so bossy! "I've disguised him," I said crossly. "And the idea's to get him to London when the Redcaps have gone."

"What about his mother? Can't she drive him somewhere in that swanky motor-car of hers?"

"I thought it best she didn't know where he was going, if they ask her. Besides, if they're looking out for motor-cars, there aren't so many with lady drivers. And they'll have seen her car outside the hospital."

She helped me back the pony into the shafts of the cart. "Tell that la-de-da Elizabeth that her plan's rotten. She's a bird-brain – that's why I'm trying to forgive her for what she did. And she's feeling guilty, that's why she's helping. Fetch the lad now. My mam's in the dairy, making butter, and Sally, the new land-girl, is helping Da with the sheep. So they won't see you. I'll come with you now – I'm supposed to be mending a fence so I can't stay long. Better leave a note for your folks, though. What'll you tell them?"

I didn't like to admit I hadn't thought what to say. Perhaps a half-truth was best.

I wrote: "*I have taken Tommy for an urgent reason. X Bea.*"

It was annoying that Jem had almost taken over the whole

idea but I did feel happier when we had been to collect Ronnie from Tanglemere. We took a side lane to avoid the Manor but had to join the village High Street. I drove, conscious of Ronnie huddled on the seat behind, almost hidden by the large purple hat, with Jem sitting opposite him, keeping a look-out.

Mrs. Rossiter was still at the hospital so I had left her a note, saying we were taking Ronnie to the Masons' farm. Then I made Mrs. Maggs and the girls promise not to talk to anyone who came to the door.

"This is a mad idea," I heard Ronnie mutter.

"Keep smiling and don't look back," Jem said suddenly and I saw the large black car outside the Rectory. I could hear Father playing the organ in the church and then saw the Vicar walking down the path from the Rectory with the two Redcaps. All of them looked serious.

I heard a faint gasp behind me as Ronnie saw them too. The Vicar waved at me and Jem made me wave back. Then the Redcaps got into their car. The church was hidden from the road by a small avenue of ancient yews but I held my breath as we passed it, in case my parents came out and saw us.

I heard a clattering of hooves behind us as we came to the lane which led to the farm. I was concentrating on driving Tommy, so it was Jem who said in a disgusted voice, "It's that Elizabeth! What's she doing following us?"

I stopped Tommy and looked round. There she was, red-faced and angry-looking. "Where's Ronnie?" she called out. "The girls said he was going to the farm. Who's that old lady and why isn't Ronnie coming to our stables?"

"Oh – shut up, you silly idiot!" Jem yelled at her.

"He's here," I said.

Ronnie peered at her from under the hat. "Why not tell the whole world I'm here!"

Elizabeth reined in her horse, and her mouth fell open with surprise. Then she went on, "Come to our stables. I've got the stuff to bleach his hair."

"It's no good," I said. "I saw the military police driving through the Manor gateway.

"Even if they didn't search the place then, they might very well later on. We'd better get on."

Tommy was peacefully eating grass but I flapped the reins and he walked on, up the rutted farm track, Elizabeth riding beside us. I thought her face wasn't nearly as pretty when it was red and sweaty.

"We'd better stop here," Jem said when we were still half way up the farm track. I could see the house and buildings in the distance; there was a stubble-field to our left and a thick overgrown bramble hedge on the right. Beyond that was the field where I'd walked through the cows, singing. It wasn't long ago and yet that girl seemed a different Bea, thinking of nothing beyond her feelings for Ronnie and Tod. The war had barely touched me then.

Jem led Tommy down the edge of the stubble-field until we were sheltered from the farm by a stand of elms. "On foot now," she said and Ronnie and I got out.

To my surprise he reached for my hand and I could feel a shiver which passed right through his body.

Elizabeth reined in her horse. "I might as well go home," she said in a small voice.

Jem opened her mouth to say something rude but I trod on her foot, hard. We needed Elizabeth's hair-bleach – I knew Jem, like myself, wouldn't have anything like that. Besides, I still didn't entirely trust Elizabeth. With her spiteful streak, she might very well drop a hint to someone that we were hiding Ronnie.

"Please come back again – Elizabeth you had that good idea of changing the colour of Ronnie's hair – we need your help badly," I said.

She sniffed. "I'll think about it," She turned her horse and cantered back the way we had come.

"Can you trust her, anyway?" Jem asked.

I didn't answer as she led us round the field to where the big barn stood a little way from the huddle of farm buildings.

Inside, fractured sunlight came through chinks in the rafters, touching the pale gold of the straw stack at the far end.

"Up here," Jem said, climbing up the bales. Ronnie followed her.

I climbed behind him and I couldn't help a nervous giggle when he tucked his skirt up, showing muscular hairy legs and long white underwear.

From the top, Jem slid down to the back of the stack, where there was a space between the straw and the wall. "Come on," she said. "Nobody will find you here – at least not for a couple of days."

"I'll fetch a blanket from the house and some bread and cheese," Jem went on.

Ronnie's face was white in the half-dark as he slumped against the bales. "There's no…" he stuttered. "Supposing I need…"

Jem laughed. "I reckon you're used to a fancy bathroom and inside lavatory. I'll bring a bucket. Have to go now or my mam will wonder where I am. I'll come back after dark with some food and a blanket." She climbed up the stack, not minding at all that her skirt rucked up, showing red woollen bloomers.

"I shall have to go too," I said "But I'll be back after dark with more food and money for the train." Some of my earnings, from working at the Rossiters – I had given part to Mother for my keep.

"I have money," he said. "Look – this is a crazy idea. We'll never get away with it. And I'm not going on a train dressed as an old lady. My feet give me away."

"We'll work that out."

Suddenly there was a distant gun-shot – probably someone shooting rabbits – but Ronnie suddenly clung to me, his whole body quivering.

I held him tenderly, like I would a child. "You see – you can't go back, can you?" I said gently.

"No." The words stuttered out, as if he had to force them. "But I'm not sure I can face running off either."

He didn't know, but I had made up my mind.

I would go with him.

I was back home, unharnessing Tommy, when I heard Bertie barking at the front door. My parents had come back and I had no idea what to say to them. If I asked permission to go with Ronnie, they would never let me but I would feel so guilty, just running away.. And what was I going to say now? Ronnie needed me and I loved him. I was sure he'd never get over his nerves and board that train for London without me. I wasn't going to stay up there, was I?

Mother came out just as I was putting the harness away in Tommy's shed. "Are you in there, Bea?" she called.

I came out, red-faced and sweating with nerves. "Why did you take Tommy out?" she asked. "Why was it so urgent?"

"I was doing an errand for the Rossiters." Then I thought someone might have seen the 'old lady' in the governess cart so I added, "Mrs. Maggs' sister was visiting and had a dizzy spell so I offered to take her home, as Mrs. Rossiter wasn't there." I hated lying to my mother and the story sounded unlikely.

Mother looked at me searchingly. "Did Oberon Rossiter pass his medical?"

"Yes," I muttered and found I was crying because I didn't want to deceive her.

Of course she thought it was because he would have to go back so she put her arm round me and made me tea. Jimmy, just home from school, was asking questions but Father just patted my shoulder. He might be blind but he knew when I was upset.

I couldn't eat much tea, pleaded tiredness and went to bed as soon as Jimmy was asleep. I'd decided the best plan was to leave the house when everyone was in bed.

Supposing someone from our village was on the train? Supposing the Redcaps or other police were waiting at Felford, where we changed for London? I needed to disguise myself as well as Ronnie. I looked in Mother's long mirror. My wild red hair would show up anywhere. I fetched her scissors and began work.

I could hear Mother reading the newspaper aloud to Father as I crossed the landing. I knew their routine. She would make cocoa, let Floss and Bertie out, and then they would go to bed.

I wrote and rewrote a note to my parents, changed into my Burlington Bertie trousers. The cap I took from Alex's room was too big but it would have to do. My head felt strangely light without my long frizzy hair and the ragged ends I'd cut tickled my neck.

At last I heard my parents come upstairs, the thud as Father took off his boots and talking softly next door. Then – silence. I put my savings and spare underclothes into a knapsack. Then I wrote the note:

Ronnie has to hide and he needs me to help him. (I felt sure this was true.). Please tell Mrs. Rossiter I am going with him to see his father in London to find a safe place. He needs me to help him. Please don't worry about me. With love, Bea.

I had to go now – or never.

I'd forgotten Bertie as I made my way downstairs carrying an oil-lamp. Every board seemed to creak and I waited for him to bark. But he only rushed out of his basket by the stove, wagging his tail. I found a heel of cheese and some of Mother's oatcakes and gave him one, putting the rest of the food into my bag.

I left the note on the kitchen table and tried not to cry when I thought how anxious and angry they would be. Ronnie had to come first.

Then I pulled up the wooden latch on the back door and went out into the night.

The stars were still bright in the sky but I still needed the oil-lamp and even so, I nearly fell on the rough edges of the plough when I came to the field..

When I walked into the barn, I saw a faint light at the far end. I slung the bag over my shoulder and just managed to hold on to the lamp as I climbed up the stack and slid down the other side.

A candle in a glass threw shadows over the hidden corner and I stopped dead at the sight of Elizabeth drying Ronnie's hair with a rough towel. There was a strong smell of bleach. Jem looked up, an enamel bowl in her hands. "I didn't think she could manage on her own." Her voice was cool.

I felt a jab of jealousy as Elizabeth put the towel down and began to arrange Ronnie's curly hair, now pale as the straw itself. "See? You'd never recognise him," she said triumphantly as he moved away. "And I've brought some of Edwin's clothes for him – they're about the same height – his Drummond kilt and tartan sash.."

"I'm not wearing a skirt again," Ronnie muttered

She turned on him but smiling. "You can be an honorary member of our Clan."

Ronnie was staring at me. I'd taken off Alex's cap because it was so big I could hardly see out. "Your hair! Your beautiful hair!!"

Elizabeth giggled. "She looks like a boy – she's skinny enough."

I wanted to kill her, yet again. "Long hair is old fashioned.– Mrs. Rossiter has the modern bob too like all the smart people in London."

At least I would never have to put my hair up with all those hatpins – and I liked the free, cool feeling with nothing tangling on my shoulders. I knew the cap would look odd with the black jacket and trousers but it would have to do.

"I don't want you to come with me. Your parents…"

"She's completely mad!" Elizabeth said. "Anyway – I have to go home or I shall be in trouble – except Mama and Papa are so wrapped in grief they may not have noticed me go out."

"I think you've lost your senses but I'll wish the both of you good luck," Jem said, surprising me with a quick hug. Then she followed Elizabeth back, up the straw-stack.

Ronnie stood facing me, holding my hands. The candlelight made his face ghost-white with dark hollows for his eyes. "I should send you home," he said.

I put my arms round him. "I just want to get you safely to London. The Redcaps will be looking for a man on his own – with dark curly hair – not for a fair-haired man with a boy – and wearing a kilt. We should sleep but leave early, for the milk train." I put my shorn head against his chest and felt his quick breathing.

His voice was low. "What have you told your parents?"

"I have asked them to tell your mother and that we will call to see your father in London. That's all"

I pulled some straw out to make a rough bed. "You need to rest."

We used my knap-sack as a pillow and covered ourselves with the old blanket Jem had brought. I wished we could lie skin to skin but it was cold and he was dead tired so we kept all our clothes on.

At first we lay side by side, like stone carvings on a tomb, but soon I turned to hold him in my arms and he laid his head on my chest.

Soon his whole body relaxed and he slept

I only dozed because it was cold and uncomfortable with straws sticking into me.

Suddenly he was screaming and I had to put my hand over

his mouth. "Blood…too much blood.."

His words made me shudder but I spoke softly to reassure him and held him as he threshed about almost as if he took a fit. Then his eyes opened and he relaxed.

"Oh dearest Bea," was all he said.

That was enough for me.

CHAPTER 19

I didn't dare risk buying a ticket, even with our disguises, so I took Ronnie through a hole in the fence and we walked up the side of the line to the platform.

It was a cold and grey dawn. We sat behind the milk churns and held hands. He wore Edwin's tweed jacket but his knees and hairy legs below the kilt looked bare and cold. He saw me looking and smiled. "I don't envy the Scots! Very draughty."

I tried to smile too. "Will you go to one of your Slade friends?" I asked him. He didn't know yet that I planned to stay with him, at least until he had found somewhere to live.

"Some are already in the Artists Rifles. Others might think it their duty to report me. I thought I would see my father and his – mistress. I've been there before. He has a studio in Hampstead but spends a great deal of time with Bunny Delgardo."

I had almost forgotten Mr. Rossiter's love, the famous variety actress – as famous as Vesta Tilley – and now I longed to meet her. Just supposing – that she found me talented and I could somehow work in the theatre? I knew I was having impossible dreams but the idea just dimmed the cold edge of a reality which meant Ronnie would always now be on the run from the Army.

"You had better buy a return ticket, Bea, my love," Ronnie said.

"We'll buy tickets in Felford, not here where we might be

recognised." I didn't tell him that I was not coming back – yet.

When the train at last rumbled in, its steam white against the almost dark sky, we managed to slip into a carriage undetected. I knew the Stationmaster was getting old and I'd heard it tell that he was often late on duty.

I remembered that other journey to see Tod and all those journeys to school – as we sat, holding hands in the empty carriage. I made up new names and a different address, should anyone ask. I tried to think of Scottish names. But he had to stick to Drummond if he wore the tartan. "You are Alan Drummond and I am your young brother Rob – and we are from – from Edinburgh, in Scotland." I warmed to the theme. "We are going to see a Variety show in London, hoping to gain an audition." I was rather pleased with myself but it wasn't hard, as that was what I would like myself.

"What a tale!" he smiled at me. "Perhaps you should take up novel-writing." It was the first time since he came back that he teased me and I was glad.

He was shivering so I hugged him close and by the time we reached the town, we were nicely warmed up.

At Falford, a bunch of Canaries, giggling and chattering, got out of another carriage and there was a noisy unloading of the milk churns. I drew Ronnie into the hurrying crowd, so we passed out of the station without anyone demanding a ticket. Then I went back and bought two tickets for London. I thought it best if I bought them and practised sounding like a teenage boy, good for my acting skills.

There were soldiers on the next train and I was careful to choose a compartment already almost full of ordinary people.

I felt quite travelled, being for the second time in the huge London station as we walked through the crowds towards the cab-stand outside. There were ordinary soldiers and people going to work – nobody took any notice of us.

Suddenly I saw them – two Redcaps, striding in our

119

direction!

"They're after me," Ronnie muttered but I took his hand and led him away, to a news-stand, where I bought two copies of *The Times*. "Here." I found an iron seat and we both opened our newspapers, hiding behind them like spies in an adventure tale.

My heart was thudding as I looked round the paper and saw the Redcaps had gone. "I suppose it's stupid – they're probably still asking for you round the village and anyway, you look quite different now."

"I look stupid!" Ronnie said.

We got a cab and Ronnie gave the man directions. Again I looked at those crowded London streets, where soldiers rubbed shoulders with people going to work – a mixture of horse-drawn cabs, motor-cars and bicycles on the road.

At last we turned off the big thoroughfare, down a narrow road and into a small, leafy square surrounded by substantial and attractive houses. "Will the maid recognise you?" I asked nervously.

"I believe she's new since I last came. Effie went to work in a factory."

Ronnie paid the cab and took me up stone steps to the front door. A little maid answered the bell. She looked surprised. "Mr. Rossiter and Madame Delgardo are breakfasting," she said. "Can I give them your names, Sir?" She was staring at Ronnie's kilt and my trousers.

I could see Ronnie hesitating. "Alan Drummond and his brother, Robert."

"Show them in!" boomed a voice.

Nothing is as you imagine. I thought Mr. Rossiter would be tall, with a long beard and wearing a painter's smock. I was right about the beard, but it was neatly pointed and he was short, wearing a kind of smoking jacket in black silk patterned with golden dragons.

And as for Bunny Delgardo – I had only seen a badly

printed small picture of her in the paper – but she was tiny, her small face dominated by large hazel eyes. She came forward and hugged Ronnie, careless of her violet silk dressing-gown, which parted a little to show an amazing pale mauve nightgown, frothing with lace.

Ronnie saw them stare at me and quickly introduced me. "Beatrice is wearing boys' clothes so we are not noticed."

Bunny hugged me and I was enveloped in the scent of honeysuckle and jasmine. Her head came just below my chin – and I am thought to be small for my age.

"You have come to help our dear Ronnie," she said. "Come and sit down and have breakfast."

We were both gritty and soot-sprinkled from the train so we asked if we could wash first. Mr. Rossiter took Ronnie off somewhere and Bunny took me upstairs to a very grand bathroom the like of which I'd never seen before, not even at the Rossiter's house. It was patterned with beautiful tiles, flower-painted and the bathtub was large, with a golden tap. The soap smelled of Bunny's scent and the towels were big and soft.

When I came down to the breakfast room, Mr. Rossiter was talking to Ronnie. He smiled at me, saying, "Your mother telephoned me last night. She guessed Ronnie would come here but she thinks the Police will come here after going to my studio – it's common knowledge that Bunny and I are – close friends. So – Ronnie – you need to find somewhere else to live." He looked at me. "And I suppose you will have to go home, Beatrice. Selina – Mrs. Rossiter – says the girls are missing you already and your mother has been round, demanding your return."

"Don't nag the poor boy and his friend now," Bunny said, smiling at us. "They both look exhausted and must need some food."

She plied us with toast, white rolls, fruit from an over-flowing bowl, tea or coffee – I daringly chose coffee, which I had not drunk before. Although I drank it, I didn't really like the strong taste.

The sunlight shafted through the plane trees outside into the light-filled room, which was dominated by a great vase of lilies. I was too tired to take much in but had the impression of subtle cream and green wall paper, cheerful flowered curtains and large, impressive paintings on the wall – I supposed they must be Mr. Rossiter's work because there was a portrait of Bunny Delgardo, bare-shouldered and in a dress so low-cut that I could see the tops of her small but rounded breasts.

I could see why Mr. Rossiter was attracted to a woman so different from his wife and after she had shown me to a cosy bedroom up another flight of stairs and told me to rest – her kind soft voice and manner made me realise she wasn't just a beauty who held people spellbound in the theatre.

She told me that Ronnie would sleep on the chaise-longue (whatever that was) in the drawing-room. "Afterwards, we make plans and you, my darling, will have to go home."

I had to tell her. "I'm so excited meeting you – my one ambition is to dance, sing and act."

She looked at me. "Have you done much singing?"

"At concerts in the village. My *Burlington Bertie* went down very well," I boasted, trying to smother yawns.

"Perhaps before you go, you can sing for me. There is a pianoforte in the drawing-room."

I went to sleep almost happy and thinking that surely, those Redcoats wouldn't find us here. I hadn't told her that I intended to stay a while, until Ronnie was settled into his new life.

CHAPTER 20

I woke up, wondering where I was. Then I remembered. We were staying with the famous Bunny Delgardo but we had to move on, or Ronnie could be in danger. I'd gone to sleep after breakfast so what time was it now?

I could hear people talking, quietly in the room below. Was it night or day? I got up and drew the curtains. It was dusk and the lamps in the square were lit but they gave out a strange blue light which glittered ghostly through the plane trees. I had heard that London lamps were covered with blue paper, so the Zeppelin pilots couldn't see them.

On my way to the bathroom, I could see a light downstairs and the voices grew louder. "She must go back," I heard Mr. Rossiter say. Ronnie answered but I couldn't hear what he said.

I washed, changed and went downstairs.

I followed the sound of voices into a drawing-room, dominated by a shining grand piano. Ronnie and his father were standing together, his father just saying, "No, you can't go back. I can see…" Then he stopped. I had an impression of heavy blue velvet curtains at the long windows and more paintings before Bunny got up from what must be the chaise longue – a kind of sofa.

"Darling!" She clasped me in her scented embrace. The ostrich feather in her little hat ticked my nose, making me sneeze. She was wearing a purple dress rather similar to the one in the portrait, low-cut and tight-waisted and when she

drew back, I saw she was wearing rouge on lips and cheeks
and her eyes were outlined with black khol. She was beautiful but quite old, at least fifty.

"Did you sleep well?" Without waiting for an answer she
went on, "I have to go to the theatre this evening. Daisy, the
maid, has left a cold supper in the dining-room. If you have
gone by the time I get back I hope we will meet again."

It was now or never. I might not get another chance to
perform in front of this great Variety Artiste. "Please – could
I sing one song to you?"

"Bea – I have to take you to the station," Ronnie said.

"Not yet," I said rather too loudly.

"Ronnie has to find lodgings where he won't be known,"
his father said.

Was I being selfish? I knew I would refuse to leave him but
just for five minutes – I could sing to Bunny Delgardo.

"Let her sing to me," she said. "I can see she is a determined
girl. Shall I play for you, darling?"

"*Burlington Bertie* – do you know it?"

Of course she did and she played opening bar. I had no top-
hat nor stick but I wouldn't let that stop me. I strutted up and
down, singing, at first nervously and then letting myself go,
imagining a big audience and a glittering, gold painted
theatre.

To my surprise, all three of them clapped and Mr. Rossiter
said, "Bravo!"

I waited, my heart thumping, for Bunny to comment. She
came over and hugged me. "Very good, darling," she said.
"You have stage presence and a great little voice – could we
sing something together? Do you know Lord Tennyson's
"*Come into the Garden Maude*?"

Of course I did – although I thought it far too sentimental.
She played the first bars and I sang with her, her deeper,
contralto voice a good contrast with my higher soprano.

Again they clapped but the sound was drowned by a loud

ringing of the door-bell.

"Are you expecting someone, darling?" Bunny asked Mr. Rossiter.

"No." He looked anxious and I saw Ronnie's hand quiver with nerves.

I ran to look through a tiny gap in the curtains. The muted blue lamp-light shone on the top of a big black car and at the same time I heard men's voices as Daisy answered the door just below us.

I felt sick as I turned to the others.

Daisy came into the room. "There are two policemen, asking for Master Ronnie."

"What did you say?" his father asked urgently.

Daisy went red. "I said I dunno where 'e was but I'd ask his father. Was that right?"

"Yes yes – where are they?"

"Downstairs, waiting in the hall, Sir."

Ronnie had gone ghost-white and when I went to hold his hand he was trembling. What could we do? Was this the end of our dreams of escape?

Ronnie's father looked alarmed. "I suppose the Army police have informed the local Bobbies that Ronnie may be here. I'll try and put them off but they may come and search the place. You'll have to hide…" He turned to Bunny. "The fire-escape…"

"Follow me quietly." She led us out of the room and up to the third floor, where she opened a door. Now I could see searchlights criss-crossing the sky and faint light gleamed on an iron stairway, twisting down into darkness. "There's a door in the garden wall. It leads out to the street. Then – get a cab in High Holborn and take Beatrice to the station. Meet me at the Gaiety Theatre, Aldwych. Ask for the Stage Manager – I will telephone him in advance. He's never met Ronnie before so you can go on being…what was it? Alan."

We hurried down the spiral steps and into a dark, walled

garden where we ran to the far side and through the gate. All the time, I was half-expecting someone would shout from the house but nothing happened.

Running through an alleyway we came to a side street and then into the big thoroughfare where Ronnie hailed a cab. "Euston Station," he told the driver.

"No. I'm not going home yet," I said. "You can't make me."

He began to argue, then the cabbie said, "Make up your minds, gents. I haven't got all night. I heard tell the Zeppelins might attack as it's full moon."

"Gaiety Theatre, Aldwych, please," I said in my new, gruff boy's voice.

The blue-muffled street lights gleamed on two police helmets as they came out of the turning to the square.

Were they after us?

CHAPTER 21

I couldn't believe I was really in the famous Gaiety Theatre in Aldwych. Ronnie had led me round the side, to the Stage Door, where Bunny's magic name wafted us past the doorman and into the bustle of back-stage.

We were told to sit in a kind of alcove with what I imagined were dressing-rooms on either side as a harassed-looking woman whose dress was decorated with pins, dashed into one room after another, carrying armfuls of clothes and two girls, dressed in low-cut, beautiful dresses, came out of another door, chatting as they passed us. Somewhere further into the theatre, an orchestra was tuning. I felt excitement spread through me, even though I was still very anxious for Ronnie. This noise, bustle and music – this was where I belonged..

At last a plump man in a black tail-coat came out of a door, saying he was the Stage Manager. "I have had a telephone call from Madame Delgardo saying the young man is a talented artist who could help paint our scenery – the flats. But she didn't say anything about another boy." He was staring first at me, and then at Ronnie.

"I'm a girl," I said in a small voice. "And I can sing."

The Stage Manager twisted the ends of his moustache and frowned. "Do you know how many girls tell me they can sing?"

I refused to give in, although he towered over me and looked so grand, in his black tail-coat and white shirt. "But I can sing…" I began but at that moment Bunny herself swept in, like a small scented tornado.

"George darling," she said to the Manager, "Do meet …er"

"Alan Drummond," Ronnie said quickly.

Bunny laughed. "Of course – my memory! Alan – he's a distant relation of mine – and a brilliant painter. Bea – I thought you were going home." Obviously she thought there was no point in my continuing the pretence of being 'Robert'.

"Not yet," I said, avoiding Ronnie's reproachful face. If only I could stay on – even running errands for such a great theatre would be something.

Bunny hung on to the Manager's arm. "Bea sings very well indeed, darling. Perhaps when she is a little older…?

The Manager looked me up and down. "So – you're disguised as a boy! Perhaps safer these days in London. Are you over sixteen?"

"Almost," I said.

"Then come for an audition – another day. Bunny thinks you have talent – so we will find out. But there are no vacancies in the chorus here."

I wanted to jump into the air with joy. I tried to forget how horrified Father would be and so unlikely to let me live in London. Mother, though, used to have ambitions to be an actress…so perhaps she might agree.

"Well, as for now, maybe you'd like to stay for the show," the Manager said. "And I think we could employ Alan, at least. We are short-handed back-stage and this production is going to run and run."

"Alan is looking for somewhere to stay, George." Bunny smiled up at the Manager. It didn't seem to matter that she was old, she looked irresistible.

"Well, if he doesn't mind roughing it, I might find him a camp bed amongst the props."

Ronnie thanked him but I felt a lowering of my spirits. It looked as if I might have to go home anyway.

The Manager asked if we would like to see the show – but

it would have to be in a mysterious place called The Gods. I could see Ronnie about to refuse, in case he was recognised but I whispered to him one word – "Please," and he gave way.

"I'll take you back in my cab," Bunny said. "Mr. Rossiter isn't here tonight – he's been to the performance several times".

So we saw the amazing musical, *"To-Night's the Night"* from seats so high up that I felt if I leaned over the rail I would dive into the packed audience.

It was the best evening of my life. There were many changes of scene and the plot held me spellbound. I was entranced by the music and colour of it all. Bunny was a good actress and her voice full and true – although she was older than many of the cast she had a kind of magic about her, which made her a star.

We could see Army officers in the audience below us so we stayed firmly in our seats during the interval. I remarked how well Bunny acted and sang.

He smiled. "I've seen her on stage before – when I came to London. She's wonderful, I agree. And I like her. Do you know, my father would like to marry her."

"Marry? You mean be divorced from your mother?" This would be such a scandal in our village. "Don't you mind?"

"Not really. I like Bunny and my parents used to quarrel a lot. I don't think my mama would be upset. She's so independent now she's gone back to nursing. She says it's more fulfilling than the stage. Actually, I believe she was finding it harder to get good parts because she was getting older."

The lights went down now and the wonderful orchestra began to play for the second act. We didn't speak again until we were hurrying down all those stairs. I felt dizzy with the wonder of it all and I hated leaving the beautiful world of make-believe.

We were mingling with the people from the better seats now,

making our way backstage when Ronnie suddenly stopped and clutched my arm. "Redcaps," he said and he literally pulled me out into the foyer and then the street.

"Back streets," he muttered, still dragging me along.

"But they won't all be after you – specially now you're hair's a different colour," I said breathlessly as he pushed his way through the crowds. "It's so unlikely that…"

He wouldn't listen but dragged me on. I heard someone say something about "Zeppelin attack," but I didn't hear where and it seemed unlikely, even though the search-lights still criss-crossed the sky and we had trouble crossing the main thoroughfare because of a huge gun on a kind of trolley, pulled by horses and manned by soldiers. People were rushing to get out of the way and there was a general feeling of panic. The blue muffled street lights made the whole scene somehow un-real and I felt as if I were in a kind of dream – or maybe a nightmare.

Ronnie took me through much quieter back streets and at one time we seemed to be running across grass – he muttered that it was Lincolns Inn Fields – I had no idea that there were fields inside London.

"Surely they won't be following us?" I panted. I'm a good runner but Ronnie was faster and I now felt tired. "Please, stop a moment."

He did and we both leaned against a wall, out of breath. I recognised the turning ahead into the Square. A pace away was an Inn, on the corner of the two streets, and the blue light shone on the sign, a picture of a sea-creature, a Dolphin. This street was almost empty but I could hear sounds of horses and occasional toots of a horn as motor-cars threaded their way through the traffic in the bigger thoroughfare. The moon had risen and competed with the moving searchlights. Was a raid expected? I hardly cared. All I wanted was to stay with Ronnie.

"I can find a cab for you in Holborn," Ronnie said. "It's near here."

It was then I finally decided. "I'm not going," I said. "I'm staying with you. We will get a message to your mother and she can tell my parents I'm well and will be staying a little while. I want to help you."

Ronnie gripped my arms so hard it hurt. "It's my choice to be a deserter. I don't want you to be involved. As I said before, you're too young."

He was sending me away with the same tiresome excuse. "But I am involved – I love you!" I cried and then I felt Ronnie turning away and he looked over my shoulder up at the sky.

I followed his gaze. The searchlights lit up an airship, like a great silver cigar, which was almost almost directly above us. I knew what it was and I couldn't breathe.

Something was falling from the Zeppelin and the next moment there was a terrific explosion which threw us both to the ground. I heard Ronnie give a muffled scream and then I was throwing off debris of glass and wood.

I was confused and it took me a moment to see Ronnie was trying to stand, holding his head. I helped him up and felt the wetness of blood. "Something hit me," he whispered. I saw huge chunks of jagged glass fallen out from the tavern window lying at his feet.

He was looking at the gaping hole in front of the Dolphin – where smoke almost hid people running out, screaming. "They need help," he said – his voice high and shaky – and before I could stop him, he was gone, into the hole.

For a moment, I couldn't get past the terrified survivors.

"You can't go in there!" A man clutched at my arm and as I was struggling with him I saw Ronnie's yellow hair through the smoke. He was pulling a body out of the Dolphin and I saw dark blood coming from his hand.

I went to help him, and tried to help him carry the body but we only gained a few feet before Ronnie collapsed. "Help

131

me!" I called out to the many people crowding round. I screamed Ronnie's name but he didn't move and now I saw a terrible sight – his face was almost hidden by a curtain of blood which was pouring from that wound in his head. He half lay across the man we had rescued and I now saw he was only about the same age as himself.

I heard myself screaming, "Don't die, don't die!" and then a big man was pulling Ronnie off the boy and I yelled at him to be careful. He felt Ronnie's pulse – "Alive but my poor Joe's in a bad way – Joe, Joe!" He was kneeling over the youth and sobbing something that sounded like, "Bloody war – my poor Joe and my poor Dolphin…"

I put my folded jacket under Ronnie's shoulders and my head on his breast to see if he was still breathing. "Find a doctor!" I shouted.

Mr. Rossiter and Bunny must be back by now and would have heard the explosion – surely they would be rushing round to see if they could help?

"Fetch the Coppers, get an ambulance – get back and give us some air!" the big man was shouting. Then I saw the street-light gleaming on the helmets of two policemen as they pushed through the crowd, waving their truncheons and telling people to stand back.

Police! Would they recognise Ronnie? But his life was more important than being caught as a deserter. I almost cried for joy when I heard him moan but I couldn't move him on my own.

The big man turned round. People had brought out oil-lamps and now he could see what a state I was in and shouted out "Anyone got a coat for the boy." Someone slung a sweat-smelling jacket over me and then, at last, I heard the fire-engine bell and there was total confusion as it arrived at the same time as ambulances tried to get through the gathered crowd.

I screamed and followed as Ronnie was lifted onto a

stretcher and tried to cling on to the side. I couldn't be left behind! "Please.." I began then everything went black.

CHAPTER 22

Where was I? I felt the wheels beneath and heard ambulance ringing its bell. I felt sick with fear – was Ronnie still alive? Muted blue lights shone through a front window but otherwise the ambulance was in darkness as it bumped through the streets of London.

I looked across and in the semi-darkness I saw a limp hand hanging over the edge of a hard shelf or bed. I leaned up and would have held his fingers but felt blood trickling down from a wound in his hand. He must have cut himself again when he went through that jagged hole. I could just see the white of his face and the dark blood staining it. "Ronnie!" I called out but he didn't answer. Was he unconscious or...? I felt for his wrist. At first I couldn't find a pulse but at last there was a faint, thready beat.

It was a nightmare journey and I felt so scared. Would Ronnie survive? And how could I hide his true name from the hospital?

At long last the motor-car stopped with a jolt.

The ambulance-men helped me out but I refused a wheelchair. The moonlight lit up the grey hospital building and the big banner hanging over the front saying, QUIET FOR THE WOUNDED.

The men fetched Ronnie out on a stretcher but I kept saying, "I'm all right, I'm all right" and they let me follow them in on foot through the people and ambulances waiting outside. The ambulance cars weren't big – so I supposed the wounded

"Joe" must be arriving with another casualty.

I was told to sit down on a hard bench in a big room, where sick people sat waiting but Ronnie was carried off to the side and I followed. A nurse tried to stop me, asking, "Are you a relative?"

"I was with him when the bomb fell," I said. My voice was shaky and she told me I should wait to be examined as well.

I watched while she examined Ronnie, who was still unconscious. Now I could see the horrific sight of the blood pouring down his face from a huge cut, starting at his scalp and right down, through one eyebrow to the corner of his mouth and blood was dripping from his right hand – again the same arm as before.

I was so scared for him and still shaking myself from the shock.

The young doctor was deadly pale with dark circles under his eyes. He sighed as he examined Ronnie. "You were with him – do you know his name, lad?" he asked.

My brain seemed shocked into slowness but I suddenly thought it would be better if the hospital didn't know even his assumed Drummond name. There might just be a chance for him finally to lose his identity here.

I knew I must look a sight – my Bertie clothes all in tatters and even the jacket left in the street but the doctor must still think me a boy. I put on my best Cockney accent, practised for a scene in Mr. Charles Dickens' *Christmas Carol* at school last winter. "I dunno his name, Sir. We was just passing the time of day in the tavern when that ruddy bomb fell."

Then the bomb scene, the blood, the confusion and my darling Ronnie lying unconscious suddenly flashed into my mind and I was sick over the doctor's polished shoes. A nurse came in and muttered angrily as she cleared it up. I wobbled and nearly fell and the doctor was making me sit down while he examined me. I tried to clutch my blood-stained shirt but he opened it to listen to my heart. "You're a girl!" he said, in a surprised voice.

I was so overcome with shame at being seen half-naked that I turned away, trying to speak with dignity, "I am an actress, dressed for a part."

The nurse was standing there, taking down notes. "What's your name, girl?" she asked me, her voice thick with suspicion. I guessed she thought I told a load of lies.

I can't think how in my muddled dazed state I thought of it but after all, I was staying at Bunny's flat and I could be her daughter. Also, there was nothing to connect a boy I had met casually at the Dolphin with Ronnie. "I'm kin to Madame Delgardo, of Red Lion Square, Holborn." Would she mind? If I hadn't been at a high pitch of fear for Ronnie, I would never have had the cheek to pretend I was related to such a great variety star.

I pretended still to be faint so I stayed while the doctor examined Ronnie. "Afraid I can't save his right thumb or fore-finger," he said to the nurse. "It looks as though something – probably glass – has sliced them through. There's also a healed wound on his shoulder and forearm."

How would he paint? Then I reminded myself he was left-handed – so he could still hold a brush. I shut my eyes as the doctor gave him an injection for the pain and then stitched his face and fingers.

The nurse tried to stop me following the gurney to the ward but I pretended I still felt faint and somehow I pushed after Ronnie and the porters into a creaking lift to the upper floor.

The ward smelled better than the one in Dover but there was still strong disinfectant, masking nastier smells and a slight whiff from a popping gas fire in the centre, fixed to an old stove. The gas-lights were turned down so I could only see huddled shapes in the beds.

"You shouldn't be here. You don't need a bed." A fierce-looking older nurse swept down the ward to the bed where a young nurse was tucking Ronnie in, so hard that I doubt he could move.

"I came in with him. A bomb fell where we stood in an Inn." This time I didn't have to pretend – I was violently shaking.

"Sit there," she ordered. "A nurse will bring you water." Then she hurried off, her heels clacking on the hard floor.

I was holding Ronnie's good hand, talking to him all the time and praying silently for his recovery – that's if God was about – I wasn't so sure – so I hardly noticed the porter and a nurse bringing a patient to the next bed.

There was a muttered conversation and I heard a strange, rattling breathing and a doctor was talking, "He was brought in from the same Zeppelin raid as the lad in the next bed. Bomb injury at a tavern. We don't know who to contact."

"He's in a very bad way... Morphia injection..."

The doctor's voice went low and I couldn't hear him. After a few minutes, both doctor and nurse moved away. I got up and looked at Joe from the tavern. Blood was seeping through the bandages that almost covered his head and his eyes were closed. A tuft of fair hair stuck out from the top of his head – hair much the same colour as Ronnie's was now. As I looked, his breathing grew louder and there was a rattle in his throat and then silence.

Was he dead? My heart thudded as I called one of the nurses, who came quickly and put her hand on the pulse in his neck. "I'm afraid he's died," she said. "I'll fetch the doctor."

I felt so sad. Ronnie had been injured trying to save Joe but death had won. Supposing it had been my dear love who had died?

I was sure the big man who owned the Dolphin would be coming in.

Then I had an idea. Could Joe and Ronnie swap identities? Would it be possible? But probably the boy had parents who would mourn him.

I heard a loud voice as the ward doors opened and the big

man came almost running in, pushing aside a nurse. He looked round the ward and then came to Ronnie's bed and looked at him, saying, "Oh – my poor boy! But at least he's alive. He's worked hard for me at the Dolphin ever since I took him from the orphanage. Where's the young man who tried to rescue him, do you know?"

I hesitated. Then I told myself this was ideal for an identity swap. Joe came from an orphanage. "He's in the next bed. I'm afraid he's just died." I burst into tears, feeling genuinely sorry and also guilty for my lies.

His red face was creased with sorrow. "This blooming war! My son was killed six months ago and I didn't even have a body to bury. I didn't want him to enlist but he said he wanted to join his pals in the same regiment. Those Generals just want cannon-fodder. Well, it doesn't look as if Joe will be working for a while yet. Anyway, I have to rebuild the front of the tavern." His voice tailed off.

Then I heard familiar voices and saw Mr. Rossiter and Bunny coming through the ward doors. I felt sick with nerves – I had to explain the deception to them before they rushed to Ronnie's bed – and I hurried up to them, waving.

"Oh you're safe! Where's Ronnie?" Mr. Rossiter asked

Bunny put her arms round me. Tears were pouring down her face. "We were so worried when you didn't get back and then we heard the bomb fall on the Dolphin and wondered if you were involved. The policeman said the casualities were being taken to the Charing Cross Hospital.".

I spoke in a whisper. "Ronnie's badly injured but he'll live. Don't tell anyone. I said I'd met him in the bar and didn't know his name." I lowered my voice. "The owner of the Dolphin Tavern thinks Ronnie is Joe, who worked for him but Joe's died."

They both looked at me, confused.

"Don't you see? It's a good chance for Ronnie to take on

Joe's identity – for always. Joe has no relations."

Bunny spoke first, in a low voice. "I know the publican – Albert Greenaway. I don't like to deceive him. Besides, Ronnie will need Joe's birth certificate and the new identity card. We shall have to tell Albert the truth."

My brilliant idea was being blown to bits. "Please please don't say anything yet," I pleaded. "And I've told them I'm related to you, Madame Delgardo. I hope you don't mind."

Bunny caught on quickly and again enveloped me in her scented embrace. "You can be my dear niece Beatrice, staying with us. But I'm still not sure…"

"I must see Ronnie." Mr. Rossiter agitatedly ran his fingers through his curly hair – so like Ronnie's.

Bunny smiled and waved at Albert Greenaway, who was walking down the long ward towards us. "We know Albert so well. Gervaise has taken his artist friends to the Dolphin and we've had meals in the snug. Albert's turned right against the war since his son was killed. I shall tell him the truth and I am sure he'll help." She walked to meet him.

Mr. Greenaway smiled and bent low over her jewelled hand. A man was calling out for a nurse and a porter passed us, wheeling a trolley, so I couldn't hear what Bunny was saying to the publican. I almost held my breath. Would Albert agree?

Mr. Rossiter looked uneasy. "It's against the law, taking someone else's identity."

"We're already in trouble, hiding a deserter." I knew I had persuade him. "If Mr. Greenaway agrees to my plan, would you be able to get Ronnie's identity card and birth certificate from home? I guess the hospital will need them before they can let the body go for burial."

"Do you expect me to bury a stranger?" Mr. Rossiter's face was angry but I was looking over his shoulder at the police-man who had walked into the ward.

My heart began to beat a tattoo. Then the ward whirled round me in a nighmare confusion of faces and noises. Again the darkness came…

I was half-conscious of faces peering at me, of the acrid smelling salts put to my nose, of Bunny arguing with the hospital and then helping me to the lift and into a cab. All the time I was trying to protest, waving my arms and hearing my tearful voice as if it belonged to someone else. "I have to stay with him," I kept saying.

I was half-lying against Bunny's soft and ample breast. She spoke gently. "You gave us all a fright and the doctor wanted to keep you in. Delayed shock, he said."

I felt as if I'd come up from a dark pit. "I wanted to stay there. What's happening? Was that policeman looking for Ronnie?"

"No. I heard him mention looting – thieves taking stuff from bombed buildings One of them must have been injured."

"But what's happening? What did Mr. Greenaway say?"

"He was upset at first but I talked him round and he's agreed to help us! I knew he would. Also, I said we would help pay for the repairs to the Dolphin. Money talks, you know. At this moment he has gone back with Albert to look for Joe's identity card from his room at the Dolphin. The cards were only issued this July so he should have it in his belongings."

"And Joe's body?"

"I have still to persuade Gervaise to bury the boy as his son. But he will." She hugged me even closer. "He's going to drive back to Tanglemere to tell his wife about Ronnie. She sounds a sensible woman, if rather bossy." Bunny's laugh was an infectious gurgle and I almost joined in although I was at heart, rather shocked that Mr. Rossiter's mistress would criticise his legal wife.

As soon as we got back, she summoned a doctor, who gave me a sleeping-draught. I tried to argue against it because I still didn't know if my plan would work but the doctor was firm and I was too weak to resist.

I woke crying from a terrible dream that I was in church and

Ronnie, not Joe, was in the coffin before the altar – then suddenly, the lid opened and Ronnie was calling "Help me!" and I saw his bandaged head rise up.

"It's all right, Beatrice. I'm here." Bunny was bending over me again, her face stripped of make-up and looking older. Light was coming through the curtains. "You've slept for twelve hours. Mr. Greenaway has very kindly been back to the hospital and says Ronnie is conscious now – and much improved. It will be hard to stop Gervaise visiting him every day but obviously, if he's to be Joe from the Dolphin, there would be no reason, except for occasional kindness."

"But I can go," I said quickly. I sat up and swung my legs to the ground, hampered by the folds of a lacey nightgown.

"Mr. Rossiter thinks you should definitely go home. He will visit your parents and tell them you're safe and well but we both think you are too young to stay here…"

I interrupted her and desperation made me raise my voice. "I'm so tired of being told I'm too young!" How could I go home, leaving Ronnie in hospital? "I'm sixteen soon. If I could just stay until he's out of hospital and finds somewhere to live. He needs me."

Bunny sighed. "I know what first love is like. And he probably does need you. I tell you what – how about my asking Gervaise – Mr. Rossiter – to get permission from your father to stay in London until Ronnie recovers?"

I thought of Father and his disapproval of the 'fast' London life and how he would never let me stay if he knew it was at the house of Mr. Rossiter's mistress.

Bunny looked at me. "You are thinking that your parents wouldn't approve of me?"

"Yes," I whispered.

She smiled. "I'm used to that attitude, Beatrice. I have an idea – nearby, a very respectable woman, Mrs. Merrydown, keeps theatrical lodgings for young women. Two of our cast are living there at the moment. I can see if she has a room for a short stay."

It was then I made a decision. Who needed me most, Ronnie or my parents? They had Jimmy and Alex might very well come on leave soon. I hated to hurt them but I wasn't just their little girl any more. Ronnie and I were going to marry as soon as he was better – I put aside the thought that he'd say I was still too young – and I would be an independent married woman. If we really could switch his identity, we could safely go back to see his mother and mine – but in the meantime I wanted to be free.

Then Bunny said gently, "Beatrice – you don't know how Ronnie himself will feel when he recovers. He had a head injury and has lost two fingers – he may not be able to work. He may be changed."

"Where are my clothes?" I asked, hearing my own voice rising with fear. "I have to go to him. I shall look after him, whatever happens!"

CHAPTER 23

If it hadn't been for Bunny and the theatre, I couldn't have endured the next days, being so worried about Ronnie.

I felt strange in the little attic room at Mrs. Merrydown's, although the girls there spoke to me kindly but I could feel they thought I was a child and they kept asking me awkward questions. I said, truthfully, that I knew Bunny Delgardo and hoped for an audition at the theatre.

Violet, the prettiest of the girls in the chorus of *To-night's the Night*, looked me up and down. "You're too short for a chorus girl and too inexperienced for acting."

I felt my old temper rising but I said nothing. I was only a few inches shorter than Violet, anyway. One day I would show them all. In the meantime, after I'd seen Ronnie in the afternoon, I befriended Perkins, who guarded the stage door, by giving him Bunny's magic name and watched the show from the side of the stage, night after night. I never grew tired of the colour, the music and the excited feeling I had, waiting for the curtain to rise and take me into another world.

Bunny had loaned me the score and I stayed up late in Mrs. Merrydown's parlour, learning the songs by heart. I had a good memory and had learned sight-reading of music at home. It took my mind off my fears that Ronnie would never recover, for he had only partially regained consciousness.

One morning Bunny told me the Stage Manager had agreed to give me an audition. "But he's looking to the future, when you are older. You need to go home very soon," she said.

"I can't go, with Ronnie so ill," I pleaded.

She looked at me with sympathy. "Then as soon as he's up and about. Now, I'll find you a dress to wear for the audition."

All her clothes were too big for me, but she delved in a cupboard and found a silver dress covered with shining sequins. "I wore it when I was younger – and a good deal thinner!" And she smiled

Her own personal hairdresser trimmed and turned my short hair into a modern style, and I looked at myself in the mirror, pouting my rouged lips and bouncing my shining chestnut bob, twisting and turning in the beautiful silver dress and its matching shoes. I wished Ronnie could see me now.

I felt sick with nerves but the Stage Manager led us to a small room, where he sat at the piano and asked me what I wanted to sing. I had the feeling he was humouring me, for Bunny's sake and that made me cross, so I was confident as I sang a few verses of the popular *A Bicycle Made for Two* with appropriate actions including riding an invisible cycle. Then I asked to sing one of the songs from *To-night's the Night* and he looked surprised when I said I didn't need to see the score. "I almost know it by heart. I've learned all the choruses."

I sang with all my might and imagined myself on that glittering stage, even finishing with a few of the dance steps.

Then I waited, my heart hammering again. Bunny was sitting with her small hands pressed together, almost as if she were praying

At last he said, "You have real talent. Come back when you are older."

"Well done," Bunny said as we went home. "I'm reminded of myself at your age."

That was praise enough but I was determined I would somehow get on the stage before too long.

Pretending to be Joe's girlfriend, I visited Ronnie every day, talking to him all the while but he was still only partially conscious. I tried to feel hopeful when on the second day he opened his eyes for a moment and said one word, "Drink." I propped him up and put a beaker to his lips and he managed to swallow before relapsing into unconsciousness. It was lucky that there were more wounded soldiers flooding into the hospital every day, so the nurses were glad of any help.

Of course, Selina Rossiter wanted to see her son but Gervaise Rossiter came back from Tanglemere to tell us that he had persuaded her to wait. It would look suspicious if a well-dressed lady hovered anxiously at the bedside of Joe, the pot-boy.

"The girls didn't quite understand," Mr. Rossiter looked drawn and pale with the worry and the double journey in Bunny's car, which had taken nearly all day. "They wanted to send Ronnie cards and fruit. And my wife at first hated the thought of burying a stranger as her son but I made her realise it was Ronnie's one chance to lead a normal life without fear of being taken prisoner." He looked at me. "She sent her best wishes to you, Beatrice, but said she hoped you would remember your duty to your parents. Now I must make arrangements to take poor Joe's body back to be buried at home. I shall be away for a few days."

I had written to my mother, explaining I was well but still visiting Ronnie in hospital and I told them about Ronnie's change of identity. I knew my father would disapprove of any deception but Mother would understand. She would also know how I felt when I added I was determined to become an actress.

Bunny realised I felt strange at the theatrical lodgings and she made me promise to come in each day to join her for her a late breakfast, as she came home so late after the show. Visiting hours at the hospital were evenings only, so she just came in once with me, the day after Ronnie had asked for water.

I had to smother a giggle when I saw her, looking rather fatter than usual in long black clothes, her face peeping out from the head-dress. "I'm a nun from Joe Hodges' Orphan-age," she announced. Then she whispered, "I have my stage clothes on underneath."

I wondered if many nuns wore black khol round their eyes and rouge on their cheeks and lips.

Mr. Greenaway came with us this time but he was clearly uncomfortable as he looked down at Ronnie, who today had relapsed into total unconsciousness. "You must miss Joe's help, now you're rebuilding the front of the Dolphin," Bunny said loudly in a stage Irish accent as a nurse was hovering nearby.

"Yes. I miss the lad all the time," Albert said. "The work's going well – it was only part of the front that blew out. We should be opening again soon."

"He was one of the best behaved lads at our orphanage," she said, sitting by the bed and shutting her eyes. "I will pray for him."

"You had me fooled a moment," Mr. Greenaway said when the nurse had gone.

"I did pray for him as well as Ronnie," Bunny said quietly. "It's not only nuns who pray, you know."

Disappointed that Ronnie hadn't even opened his eyes this time, I managed to find a senior nurse and ask how 'Joe Hodges' was faring. She said his wound was healing well but they were as concerned about his half-conscious state as I was.

"You visit him every day – is he your boy-friend?" she asked.

I nodded, hoping she wouldn't ask any more questions.

The next day, Bunny gave me a letter from my mother. I recognised her neat, slanting handwriting and for a moment I didn't want to open it.

"*Dearest Beatrice,*" she wrote.
"*I am so sorry you were involved in this bomb attack and Ronnie was injured. I am praying for his recovery*

and I hope very much you will come home. Your father thinks you are far too young to think of staying in London and he is not happy at your idea of becoming an actress. I make no comment myself except I understand why Ronnie felt he couldn't go back to the trenches.

Jem tells me Tod still has nightmares although he is now walking about on crutches. She says he is greatly helped by Sally, their Land Girl, who is a caring and cheerful young lady.

I know if our dear Alex came back wounded I would do almost anything to keep him at home but I do not say this to your father. We have not heard from him lately although we sent him a parcel.

Please come home soon. Your loving Mother.

Who needed me most? Ronnie or my parents? They were anxious about Alex but my being there wouldn't really make much difference, or so I argued to myself. They were busy with Father's music lessons and Jimmy's pranks – surely they could spare me for a while? I knew, in my heart, that I was being unkind to them and yet – I had to help Ronnie. Now I was almost a woman, I realised you didn't just choose between right and wrong, black or white – there were plenty of grey areas.

CHAPTER 24

Bunny insisted on my taking a cab to the hospital each day and almost forced me to take some money. My own small stock had dwindled right down so I had to accept but one early evening I felt so low that I thought I would walk there.

I had been too worried about Ronnie to see much of London but now I walked down the back streets, asking my way to the famous Trafalgar Square – which I had seen briefly from the cab.

I got lost once but forced myself to ask a policeman – I knew Ronnie wouldn't be arrested now but I still felt anxious if I saw policemen.

He smiled in a friendly way and directed me. It was almost sunset and the sky was streaked with gold and red above the buildings and a flock of starlings were chattering and wheeling high above the famous Nelson's column. Their calls reminded me of home and I felt a pang of longing as I remembered seeing the geese flying over the river on that fateful evening when I first met my true love.

Pigeons flocked down to take food from an old man and some ragged barefoot boys were kicking a can near the famous lions, making the pigeons fly into the air. I saw a boy take aim with his catapult and a pigeon flopped down at my feet.

I shouted but the boys had seen a policeman and were running off. Then I picked up the bird. It was still warm and I remembered the dove at Tanglemere.

As I put it down, I saw blood oozing from its soft grey breast.

I found myself running, across the Square, tears blinding my eyes. I was sure this was a sign that Ronnie's condition had deteriorated and I was nearly hit by an omnibus as I dashed across the road.

Stretchers were being carried from an ambulance into the hospital and I saw soldiers, some calling out, but others white-faced and silent. When I'd passed Charing Cross station in the cab I'd seen the wounded soldiers arriving from the train.

I thought of Alex – and the dangers he faced. I had hardly thought of him except when I read my mother's letter – my darling Ronnie had filled my whole mind. Somehow, though, I felt my confident brother would always be a survivor.

All this went through my mind as I hurried to the ward, rudely pushing through the other relations waiting outside and taking no notice of a nurse calling out to me. I was sure the dead bird was an omen.

Ronnie was sitting propped up in bed.

I stood quite still, just for a moment. The dressings and bandages had been taken off his face and head and now I saw the long wound held together by stitches – a ridge that went from his scalp down one side of his face, puckering the skin round one eye and slicing through the corner of his mouth, so that side was drawn up in a strange half-smile.

I only hesitated a moment but he noticed. His voice was low and halting as he said, "Darling Bea. I know I look a sight. I made them bring a mirror. They say it will probably improve with time. And the glass sliced through my thumb and fore-finger."

I bent low over him as his voice faltered. "Ironic," he said. "The fingers being on my wounded arm but so lucky, not my painting hand."

"You're conscious and getting better – that's all I care!" I cried and in a moment I was kissing his poor mouth, not

149

caring that a nurse was nearby.

"I didn't know where I was – it was early this morning – then they kept calling me Joe Hodges," he whispered. "Why?"

"That's your name now. I'm a girl you met at the Dolphin when you worked there," I whispered back and I told him how he'd got a new identity.

"So – I'm a new man. Reborn." His twisted smile looked sarcastic.

"You're safe now." I sat very close and took his good hand – the other was still bandaged.

He made a feeble attempt to pull away. "Bea – you should be going home. You've done your best to help me."

"You're sending me away? Don't you love me any more?" I felt my cheeks wet with more tears.

"Yes – I do. But you're a lovely girl. You could be free to look for another sweetheart – someone who didn't look a freak." I had to listen carefully because his voice was still weak. "I saw the look on your face when you saw me just now."

How could I convince him? "I was shocked – yes. But your face doesn't matter. It's you I love."

"You will change your mind…" His voice tailed off and he lay back on the pillows, shutting his eyes.

A nurse came up. "Mr. Hodges needs to rest now," she snapped.

So I had to leave before the end of visiting time. I was in a strange mood. I was so happy Ronnie was getting better – but supposing he insisted I went home? I was sure he would stay in London and be employed by the theatre.

To cheer myself, I walked back up the Strand to Aldwych, lingering at the stage door. The performance wouldn't start yet but I just wanted to hide myself in the welcoming bustle and smell of greasepaint.

Old Perkins, the Doorman, let me in. I could hear a kind of wailing from one of the dressing-rooms. Perkins nodded at me. "Evening, Miss Beatrice. That noise is Miss Violet. She was rehearsing earlier and she fell, twisting her ankle. She can't go on tonight. I'm calling her a cab."

So the chorus was one girl short and I knew the songs by heart. "Is Madame Delgardo here yet?" I asked.

"She's in her dressing-room."

I found Bunny sitting at the big mirror, fiddling with her hair. She saw my reflection as I came in. "Bea! You're back early from the hospital."

"He's sitting up and talking!" I gabbled. "And I've just heard Violet's hurt herself. I know all the songs by heart and I know every bit of the performance. Please could I stand in, just tonight?"

She looked at me carefully. "Well, there's no understudy. They usually manage if one drops out. But I could ask the Manager. He was impressed at your audition but he would be doing us a great favour as you're not in the cast."

All at once I was seized with nerves. Would he agree?

This was my big chance – but it could go horribly wrong.

CHAPTER 25

Violet's friend, Liza, prodded my shoulder. "Oh – so they're putting kiddies on the stage now, are they? Lucky little Beatrice being related to Madame Delgardo."

My face burned under the stage make-up as I sat in the dressing-room while the same harassed-looking Dresser I'd seen before tried to find a wig small enough for me, to cover my too-short hair. My face looked strange, my cheeks and lips rosy with stage make-up and my eyes ringed with black khol.

Jem had long ago taught me to stand up for myself at school. Now, I said, "Oh yes, Madame Delgardo's related to my fiancé." It wasn't true and also, I had forgotten that my fiancé was Joe Hodges, but I didn't think spiteful Liza would remember.

I felt sick. Supposing I threw up over one of the illustrious actors? Or I might stumble and push into one of the chorus-girls. If I made a mistake, I would let Bunny down.

She came in and gave me a hug. "Good luck!" she said. "You look marvellous, Bea darling."

Then it was all hustle and bustle as we were hurried back-stage.

I could hear my heart beating in my ears as the orchestra struck up for the opening chorus, "*Life is very jolly down at Maidenhead.*" I didn't feel jolly at all but I pasted a smile on my face and went on with the others, Violet's friend giving me a vicious jab in the ribs to cheer me on.

The next two hours were wonderful – and they were

terrifying. I struggled to remember all those performances I had seen before, for once glad that our school had made me memorise long poems and Bible readings – because I was almost word-perfect. I was directed to the back of the chorus – I suppose they thought I'd not be noticed there if I made mistakes.

But I had forgotten my nerves – I wasn't just in the back of the chorus, I was an Actress – in a great Variety show – on a London stage and it felt like a dream, from which I hoped not to wake.

The footlights made the audience into anonymous white-faced dark shapes but they clapped, shouted and threw flowers onto the stage at the end and we took five curtain-calls!

Afterwards, I wanted to linger but Bunny hustled me out to a cab. There were well-dressed men in top-hats waiting at the stage door and one tried to give her a bunch of red roses.

She smiled at him but drew me away. "We call them Stage Door Johnnies!" She laughed. "I'm taking you home for supper tonight and you can stay with me. I hear Violet will be laid up for at least a week and the Manager has just spoken to me – he wondered if you could take her place for that time. You will have to come to rehearsals, of course, and you are too young to be on the payroll. But I wonder..."

I knew she was going to talk about my age and going home. Nothing would make me go home now I was really part of the theatre.

"Oh YES!" I said, so loudly that the cabbie turned to look at me. "And I'll be sixteen this time next week."

Mr. Rossiter had driven back again to Tanglemere, to arrange the funeral of the real Joe Hodges – under Ronnie's name, so Bunny obviously felt it was quite proper for me to stay at her house all that glorious week.

All this meant little compared to my joy at Ronnie's recovery. He left the hospital and settled in at the theatre, sleeping on a camp bed surrounded by props and bits of scenery. He was given the job of checking the box-office returns but as soon as he was stronger, he would start renovating and painting the 'flats' as the scenery was called. The first time he watched the show, he waited outside the dressing-rooms.

As I came out with the girls, I knew they were all looking at his scarred face and his one-sided smile. Just for a second, I wished he had kept his handsome looks, when they would have envied me – but I dismissed the thought, running up to kiss him. I heard the girls giggling.

When we were outside the theatre he said, "You looked – kind of radiant, on the stage," he said. "As for me…"

I stopped, taking no notice of the people hurrying past – drawing him into a narrow alley-way I put my arms round him. At first I felt his body rigid, then he began to kiss me, knocking off my hat as his mouth moved down, starting at my forehead, then both eyes, then my mouth, long and lingering. I felt the ridge of stitches down his face but it didn't matter – his kisses still set my body on fire. I'd thought being on stage was a wonderful dream but Ronnie's love filled me with even bigger joy – and longing.

"Come back to Bunny's house with me," I said. "She's having supper with some of the cast. The maid will let us in."

He drew back. "Don't tempt me, Bea. You're…"

I interrupted him. "Too young! I'm not – I'll be sixteen in two days' time."

"So old!" He was teasing me now as he led me back to Aldwych and flagged down a cab.

It was dark and fusty-smelling inside but I didn't care. Perhaps I really was a brazen hussy, as my Father would have said, but I almost melted into his arms, holding him close. Clothing, buttons, my corset – all fought against our bodies and I longed to be free of them as I nuzzled into his neck, glorying in his slight musky scent, almost overlaid with the smell of the 'theatre – men's cigar-smoke and the traces of grease-paint on my own face.

"I should go back," he said, when we jolted over the cobbles into Red Lion Square.

I pleaded with him. "Please – just stay for a little while. Bunny will be pleased to see you when she gets back." I wasn't at all sure about that. Bunny had been giving me veiled lectures, that I shouldn't get too fond of Ronnie, there were temptations in such closeness and anyway, I was going home soon, wasn't I?

I was fond of her but I thought to myself that it was my life, not hers. She might love Ronnie's father but she had forgotten what it was like to be young, to be totally filled with love and desire.

The new young maid, Daisy, stared at Ronnie's face as she let us in. He had only once been back to the house since he left hospital, to fetch the clothes his father had brought from home – as he had nothing to wear but torn and blood-stained garments. It had been Daisy's day off that time.

"Mr. Hodges works for the theatre," I explained rather unnecessarily and I asked her to bring us tea and sandwiches.

She looked at Ronnie again with that curious and yet slightly revolted expression I'd seen on others' faces. It made me angry but Ronnie said he was getting used to it.

I had not yet become used to the salty taste of Gentleman's Relish but Ronnie ate ravenously, saying he'd only shared a small pie with the Call-boy for his luncheon.

We drank the tea and ate in silence – I knew he was as worried as I that Bunny and Mr. Rossiter would come back early. When we'd finished, he drew me over to the satin-covered chaise-longue and we kissed, exchanging the taste of anchovies from the Gentleman's Relish.

Ronnie drew back. "It's no good here. I keep feeling my father will walk in. I have to go."

I nodded miserably but came downstairs with him. When

we were outside, on the stone steps, he suddenly hugged me close, "Oh Beata Beatrix!" he muttered and with a single thought we walked across the road and opened the gate into the Square gardens.

I could smell cold earth, rotting leaves and I saw the dark outlines of the plane trees. Traffic rumbled distantly in Holborn and an owl was calling in the gardens. It was a starlight night, this time with only a slice of moon in the sky, competing again with the criss-cross searchlights. Somehow I found myself leaning against a tree and he was said how much he loved me.

"So you are wearing my ring – on a chain," he murmured. "I want to see it on your hand. Will you…" We both jumped as we heard the unmistakable sound of Bunny's little motor-car, the only one in the Square, back-firing like a gun before stopping with a squeal of brakes outside the house.

"My father must have come back from Tanglemere." Ronnie said as we drew apart, almost as if Mr. Rossiter could see through the trees. "We'll have to go. If we don't go back, he will tell Bunny you weren't in the house when he arrived."

So my wonderful evening came to an end.

CHAPTER 26

Violet was better. She would be in the chorus again from next Monday and this was my last evening in *To-night's the Night*. I felt like crying but Bunny told me I'd made a good impression on the Manager and he thought I might – only might – have a career in on the stage, given time and much practise.

Ronnie hinted at a surprise for me after the show and I hoped – with all my heart – that he would say he couldn't live without me and we would marry now and live anywhere, although I had doubts about honeymoon joys on his camp-bed back-stage.

It was the morning of my sixteenth birthday. I came from Mrs. Merryweather's to the late breakfast at Bunny's. I found two presents by my plate, carefully wrapped in brown paper. I saw one was addressed in my mother's bold handwriting – so they had forgiven me for staying on in London.

Bunny sipped black coffee as she watched me open it.

I brought out a beautiful shawl, embroidered with birds and flowers and I knew at once she had made it because her favourite bird and mine, the kingfisher, was in the repeated pattern. The letter was short.

> *"Dearest Beatrice,*
> *Your father and I send you our love on your sixteenth birthday. Mrs Rossiter has told me of your stage appearances. I know it will make you happy but please don't let your head be turned as your father is still*

against the stage as a career. In future when you are older, I may be able to persuade him but now, he misses you and we both want you to come home.

We have no news from Alexander – but perhaps no news is good news, as they say.

From your loving Mother.

I cried as I showed the letter to Bunny. "Patience, darling," she said. "Rome wasn't built in a day. Now open the other present…"

She had given me a beautiful aquamarine silk blouse with frills round the neck and wrists. The colour reminded me of that dress I had worn to Elizabeth's party, so long ago. I got up and gave her a huge hug.

She kissed me. "Wear it tonight, darling. I am taking you off to supper after the show."

How could I tell her that I wanted to be with Ronnie on my birthday evening? She had been so kind that it would be rude to refuse.

I'd hoped he might have sent round a present but I knew he was trying to manage on the small wages from the theatre, and be independent from his father. "I have to live as Joe Hodges would," he said.

The last rehearsal went all too quickly and I was pleased, afterwards, when two of the girls said I'd done well and they'd miss me. "That Violet puts on airs and graces – thinks she's top-hole 'an all," Mimi whispered, just out of range of spiteful Liza.

I tried to lose myself in the show but I couldn't forget I was leaving it.

I thought I'd be dining at the theatre but Bunny whisked me away in a cab to the famous Café Royal in Regents Street. A man in bright livery helped us out and we went to a table in a softly-lit room, where candles gleamed on silver cutlery, damask tablecloths and beautiful flower arrangements. A discreet murmur of conversation came from the occupied tables. Ronnie and his father were waiting at a table in a quiet corner and they stood up smiling at me, as we came in.

"Happy birthday!" Mr. Rossiter said and my dearest Ronnie actually kissed my hand, as if I were a Princess.

I floated through the wonderful dream-like evening. There was champagne, which I liked better than lemonade and would have had more, only Mr. Rossiter waved the waitress away from me.

There were delicate courses of most delicious food, which I was almost too excited to eat, and to crown it all, at the end a waiter came in with a birthday cake glowing with candles. People at other tables saw it and someone clapped – then others in the room joined in, even the waiters. I knew I was blushing as I blew the candles out, making one wish – to live with Ronnie and act on the stage.

"Happy birthday, darling Bea," Ronnie said quietly and he handed me a small jewel-case.

I opened the velvet-covered box. It was a broach in the form of a silver heart, set with small pearls surrounding a glowing red stone I guessed was a ruby.

All I could say, was "Oh – how lovely!"

"Shall I pin it on your blouse?" Ronnie asked.

"Yes."

I felt dizzy with his nearness as he bent over me, pinning the broach to one side of the blouse, fumbling a little with his injured hand, as he had during the meal. I had been careful not to watch as he tried to hold his fork between two fingers.

"I hope you'll remember me, Bea darling, when you put this on," he said softly.

Remember him? I wanted to stay with him always. Was he still intent on sending me home? And how had he afforded this beautiful broach? Perhaps he had at last accepted the allowance his father had offered, as he was earning little at the theatre.

159

Bunny was smiling and Mr. Rossiter said, "The broach used to belong to my mother. He asked me to bring it back with me."

So Ronnie hadn't chosen it himself. I was disappointed for a moment but then I thought of Mrs. Rossiter. "Doesn't…" I hesitated – "Doesn't Mrs. Rossiter want to wear it?"

He glanced at Bunny, who was a-glitter with a magnificent diamond necklace and matching earrings, no doubt his gift to her. "No – she seldom wears jewellery. And she's fond of you, Beatrice. She said she was so grateful for all you have done – for Ronnie – that she wanted you to have the broach."

Did she realise that Ronnie and I were secretly engaged to marry? However modern and free-thinking she might be, wouldn't she want a better match for her only son than the daughter of a poor music-teacher?

He had moved his chair nearer to mine to put on the broach. Now he put his hand lightly on my knee. The damask table-cloth hid his hand from view but I knew I was blushing again. "Always remember you have my heart," Ronnie whispered.

Three young men who had just sat down at the next table were looking our way.

I felt Ronnie's hand withdraw. "I know that chap – the one with black hair and a moustache," he whispered. "Colin Campbell was at the Slade with me. He wanted to fight but he has a heart defect. I must go…"

Bunny put out her hand as he began to rise. "You're so changed he won't recognise you," she said.

My heart thudded as Colin Campbell came over to our table. The blond hair and the puckered scar certainly changed Ronnie's face but was that enough?

He was smiling at Mr. Rossiter and gave a small bow. "Sir – I recognised you, Mr. Gervaise Rossiter – and I would like to salute a great portrait painter." I saw he was only a little older than Ronnie and also slightly drunk. "I used to know your son but he joined up. Have you any news of him?"

Ronnie sat frozen in his seat and I tried to smile but I was too nervous.

Mr. Rossiter cleared his throat and fingered his beard nervously. Then he said, "I'm sorry to say he was wounded and died."

Colin Campbell moved back a step. "I'm so sorry – he's not the first from the Slade to die. He was one of the youngest students and he had great talent. How terrible for you, Sir." He looked at me. "At least you have your beautiful daughter to console you."

Bunny glanced at me, smiling. "Beatrice is my niece. Joe – her young man," and she nodded at Ronnie – was injured in a Zeppelin attack. We're hoping Beatrice's birthday dinner will cheer him up."

"I am sure it will. He's a lucky man to have such a beautiful fiancée. Forgive my interruption, Sir," and he went back to his table, walking somewhat unsteadily.

Mr. Rossiter said quietly, "It was hard to lie – to say my son was dead."

Bunny smiled. "But we know now he's safe. That's all that matters. Nobody will ever recognise him."

I could feel Ronnie was still uneasy as he looked down at his untasted slice of cake.

"Time to go," His father beckoned to the waiter.

As we walked out, Ronnie whispered, "Colin's looking at us."

I didn't tell him that I thought Colin was looking at me. I'd seen myself in the great mirrors inside the restaurant – and I knew I looked very attractive and older than sixteen. After all, I was a young lady now, who had started a glittering stage career – and I was no longer an innocent girl but a woman in love.

We stood in the foyer. It had been raining and the shops in Regent Street all had different coloured paper over their lights, reflecting rainbow colours in the puddles.

"We can share a cab and I'll drop Ronnie off at the theatre," Mr. Rossiter said.

Ronnie grasped my hand. "I need to walk – now I feel better. Would you like me to walk you home, Bea?"

"Yes," I said.

Protesting, they let us go.

Fog swirled down as we walked hand in hand through the back streets. "You can smell it's Covent Garden, can't you?" Ronnie said as we passed close to the huge warehouse where men carrying lamps were already unpacking boxes of fruit and flowers.

"I used to try to block out the stench of putrefying flesh in the Army Clearing Station by remembering the smell of flowers," Ronnie said suddenly. "I suppose I was luckier than some, not having to walk on dead bodies in the trenches, not facing gas attacks and the terror of running straight into enemy gunfire. But I can't forget those dying men – we saved some but we couldn't stop the gangrene except by amputation. Then my ambulance was shelled." He stopped. "I'm sorry. This isn't right for you to hear. But I still have nightmares."

He'd not talked like this before. I felt he had been down a path I would never know and this somehow separated us.

It was hard to see the way through the fog but Ronnie led me out of a narrow road and I felt soft turf under my feet. "Do you remember Lincoln's Inn Fields?" he said.

"Yes. And now nobody can see us," I said.

"We're invisible." He stood still and put his arms round me, kissing me passionately. Then he threw his coat on the ground and drew me down beside him. We lay close, stroking each other and the kisses grew deep and long so I felt his tongue touching mine. I was aching somewhere deep inside, filled with longing as his hand crept under my skirt and petticoat.

Then he rolled away from me and got up. "I don't want you like this." His voice was jerky. "No – you are still so young. I can't…" The fog got into his throat and he was coughing.

"We have to get back," he said at last. "I suppose you'll be at Bunny's tonight – not the theatrical lodgings?"

I felt frustrated tears coming to my eyes and he almost marched me home. We were passing the Dolphin and I saw lights through the fog and heard men laughing. "The front of the Dolphin is roughly mended already," Ronnie said. "I went to see Albert Greenaway, to thank him for my new identity."

As we came into Red Lion Square a cold wind swirled the dead leaves round our feet and the fog began to dissolve into fine rain.

"I won't come in," he said when we were on Bunny's doorstep. "They'll be back by now."

"I wish…" I began but his kiss stopped my lips.

"So do I," he murmured. "We just have to be patient."

I loved him so much but now I wanted to shake him. Why did we have to wait? "We could go to that Scottish place – Gretna – and get married. Then I could share your room in the theatre."

I could just see his face in the blue lamplight. He was smiling, patronising me. After all, he was only two years older than I was. Why did he have to put on this fatherly act?

He stroked my hair. "Darling Beatrice – all I have is a dusty room full of props and a narrow camp bed. I think you deserve something better."

"Your father paid for your lodgings when you were at the Slade. Why do you have to be so independent now?" My voice was high and unpleasant but I couldn't stop myself.

He moved a little away from me. "I'm lucky enough to start a new life with a new name. I want to be independent and I still have to be careful not to be associated with my papa. Today was risky. If I'm seen with him too often, someone might recognise me."

"You don't love me enough." I knew I wasn't being fair but I didn't care. I had to be with him.

Then the front door was flying open and Bunny stood there.

"Come in, you poor wet darlings," she said in her husky voice.

"No – thank you. I must get back. Goodnight." And he almost ran from the Square.

Stifling my tears, I refused Bunny's offer of hot chocolate and went to bed, hearing the murmur of voices below. She and Gervaise Rossiter were probably discussing Ronnie and me, I thought angrily. At any moment they would force me to go home. Well, I wasn't going. I would persuade Ronnie to run off and get married. Then I could help him pay for rooms by working in the theatre – if they wouldn't have me in the chorus again I could help with the props, with the Box Office or even sell programmes.

It was a long time before I went to sleep.

Chapter 27

"Are you awake?"

Bunny's voice. She never got up before ten so I had slept late.

She came in, holding a brown envelope. "A telegram arrived for you. I worry that it's bad news."

I took it with trembling fingers, fearing that illness or even death had come to someone at home.

REGRET ALEX IS MISSING BELIEVED KILLED.
PLEASE COME HOME. MOTHER.

Alex – I hadn't even thought of him lately – and he had been facing worse dangers than Ronnie or Tod. I was unable to move for guilt. I'd wished him away from home and now – I would never see him again. My parents and Jimmy must be devastated.

"I have to go home," I said.

"Mr. Rossiter is here. He says he will drive you in my car. The trains are packed with soldiers and a motor-car will be quicker."

"Ronnie…" I began. Then I thought he had almost rejected me last night. I had to think of my parents before anything else.

It was a horrible journey. The car had a canvas hood but the rain pushed through the side flaps, so we were both soaked and cold. When Mr. Rossiter stopped to fill the tank with more petrol he made me sip a little whiskey from a flask but I couldn't eat the sandwiches Bunny had given us.

I tried not to cry. Mr. Rossiter was silent with concentration, as we avoided Army lorries, steam tractors and a few motor-cars. We had to go slowly to overtake horse-drawn vehicles as he said the horses could take fright.

He made one remark, "It's a terrible loss for you all. You will have to be brave for your parents."

I have no idea how long the journey took but it seemed like hours. When at last we drew up outside our cottage, I was so cramped and cold that he had to help me out.

"Thank you for helping Ronnie and making him happy," he said. "Hold fast to your love."

Then he cranked the gear handle and was off while I was still hesitating outside our door. I could hear Father playing the piano, loudly. I was so used to London doors being locked that I forgot that we seldom locked ours, and knocked on the worn wood. Bertie began barking and Jimmy opened the door, a slice of bread and jam in his hand. Bertie jumped at me, nearly knocking me over as he licked my face.

"It's Taddy – our Bea!" Jimmy called out. "Bertie remembers her."

In a moment Mother was there and I fell into her arms, crying.

"Oh Bea," was all she said as she drew me inside to sit at the kitchen table.

Father came slowly into the room and felt my face. "Tears won't bring him back," he said sadly. "The Bible says 'those who live by the sword shall die by the sword' and so many are dying. Even that patriot Rudyard Kipling has changed his views since his son was killed. Europe has become a blood-bath…"

"David – remember Jimmy," Mother said but it was too late.

Jimmy threw his bread to Bertie and ran out of the room muttering, "Alex died a hero!"

For the next week I tried to help all I could. Apparently Alex – or what was left of his body – had been buried in Flanders but the Vicar had agreed to a quiet service, remembering his life. It all seemed so unreal. I went into Alex's shed and expected him to burst in at any moment, telling me off for being there. I did cry then and I felt sad that we'd never really got on and guilty that I'd wanted him to leave home.

I made Mother rest while I drove Tommy, taking Father to his music lessons, and I tried to explain to Jimmy how he must help our parents and stop being so angry.

But I was angry, too – with myself and with the war. My brother was gone and our lives would never be the same. I wanted Ronnie at my side so much that it hurt.

Elizabeth came round, white-faced and tearful. "It was all my fault with that stupid white feather," she muttered when we were alone. "And you must be doubly sad with Ronnie dead too. I went to the funeral last week. It seems dreadful that he fought in Flanders, then escaped from the Military Police only to be killed in a Zeppelin attack."

Now – what could I say? My parents and Ronnie's were the only people who knew the truth. Could I trust Elizabeth? And what was I going to say to Tod and Jem?

"I'm so sorry and I did hope I'd helped to save Ronnie," Elizabeth gabbled on, wringing her hands in a strange gesture I'd only read about. "I refused to go back to my boarding-school – all those useless, frivolous girls – and I'm working at the Manor Hospital with Jem. My parents have just got to get used to the idea of my being a nurse. They probably don't care anyway, as Edwin always meant more to them than me. But I still feel so guilty about that awful thing I did – I don't sleep well. Ronnie and Alex dead and poor Tod crippled and all my fault!" Her voice rose hysterically.

We were alone in the kitchen as my mother was by the piano, reading out a new music score for Father to learn by heart, as of course he couldn't read it.

Suddenly I was so sorry for her that I got up and hugged her. She went on crying, into the rough apron I was wearing. I knew I had to tell her. I had to trust her not to tell anyone and anyway, I wasn't going to give away Ronnie's new name. "You have to promise never to say anything to anyone."

"I promise." Her voice was muffled.

"Ronnie's alive and well but he has a new identity – not the one we made up but a proper one, with papers to prove it. I can't say any more than that."

"Oh – Bea!" She was up and hugging me delightedly. "That's wonderful. Are you still ...will you get engaged?"

I still kept the ring hidden, partly because Mother thought it best – Father was so sad about Alex that to tell him about my engagement would be unsuitable. I pulled the thin silver chain out from my dress and showed Elizabeth – and I fetched the pearl and ruby heart out of my drawer. "Wonderful," she said. "I must admit, I'm jealous. Ronnie's so good-looking. When I first met him, I hoped he might come to be fond of me."

I wondered if she would be so attracted to his scarred face and maimed hand. "Nothing's certain," I added. "He's in London and I've got to help my parents and Jimmy. I miss him so." It was my turn to cry then.

The next day, Mrs. Rossiter came round to the cottage. She was wearing a dark purple outfit, I suppose instead of the usual black mourning. My parents and Jimmy were in church for choir practice – they had insisted that life should go on as usual.

It was a dreary, wet day and I was doing the ironing in the kitchen. I knew I ought to have been to see Ronnie's mother as soon as I got back but I'd put it off.

She insisted on sitting in the warm kitchen. "It's so cosy here." Bertie and Floss were asleep together in front of the range and she sat in the rocking-chair. "I have already been here to give my condolences to your parents. It's a bitter blow, to lose a fine son like Alex and you must miss your brother

168

enormously."

I nodded. The guilty truth was I missed Ronnie far more and wished I could talk to him. I had already sent him a letter, carefully addressed to Joe Hodges, c/o the Gaiety Theatre, Aldwych and another to Bunny's house, but he hadn't replied. I lay awake at night wondering if he had changed his mind about our engagement. He could be thinking of all the obstacles to our marriage: my being so young, his disfigurement and lack of money, to say nothing of asking my father's permission.

We were sitting quite close in front of the fire and now Mrs. Rossiter leaned forward and tapped me on the knee. "Beatrice, I have to thank you so much, my dear, for all you have done for Ronnie. I am going to London tomorrow to see him – we all think it better if he doesn't come back here just now, but perhaps later and not to stay at our house. Once the war is over, of course..." She stopped. "I have talked to him on the telephone and he sends his condolences for Alex's death – and his love to you. Do your parents know how fond you are of each other?"

"Mother knows. Father has retreated into his music since Alex died. I haven't said anything to him. Oh, I do miss Ronnie so much!" This burst out of me – I hadn't intended to say anything – in case he had changed his mind.

She smiled. "First love is very strong. But it can lead you astray. I felt like that before I married Gervaise but now we have drifted apart."

I thought of Bunny.

She sighed. "Enough of that. Time will tell. Now, the girls want you to come back. Could your mother spare you at this sad time?"

"Do the girls know about Ronnie?"

"I couldn't let them think he was dead. I've sworn them to secrecy and I certainly haven't told Mrs. Maggs nor anyone else that we buried another young man. So – will you come?"

"I'll ask my mother if she can spare me." I wondered if I could bear to go into the studio, filled with those memories of Ronnie painting my portrait. But being at Tanglemere would be one step nearer to him.

Mother agreed and said it would do me good to get away from home. First, though, I had to see Jem and Tod. The Masons had written a letter of condolence but Jem hadn't been to see me although village gossip would have told her I was back.

Elizabeth had told me Jem was working full-time at the Manor Hospital, now her father had the Land Girl to help on the farm, and I wondered why she'd left the High School. She would need to learn more human biology if she was to become a doctor.

I walked over to Berry Farm on Sunday afternoon. It was a day of scurrying clouds and shafts of winter sunshine which made the last leaves glow on the trees. I could hardly believe I was the same Bea Denning who had walked round with a milk jug, earlier in the year. I'd been absorbed by my own ambitions and life and had hardly thought of the war – which seemed so far away then that it could never touch me.

The cows were sheltering from the wind, clustered by the trees, and took no notice at all of me.

"I'll fetch Jem. She's at her books, upstairs," Mrs. Mason said. "She's ever so determined to be a doctor, you know." Her round rosy face creased into sadness. "We're that upset about your Alex, dear. I brought round a pie for your Mam when I heard."

Jem and I stared at each other – then she gave me a bear-hug, so hard that I thought my ribs might crack. "So flipping terrible for you," she began

I interrupted. "I've something to tell you. Shall we walk down to the dairy?"

I was sure that Jem would keep my secret so I explained what had happened – again, as with Elizabeth, I didn't give her his new name. Time for that later, when he felt really safe.

She clapped me on the shoulder – so hard I reeled back. "He couldn't have gone back. I'm glad. I'm so thankful that Tod gave himself a 'Blighty' as they call it, putting his foot under the wheel. He says he was lucky they believed it was an accident as other men were found out – and faced the firing squad."

"How is he?"

"Come and see for yourself. He's in the stable."

I breathed in the familiar smell of horse and hay. Tod was in a loosebox, propped up on one crutch grooming a shining black filly. I felt a jolt from the past when I saw she had a small white mark on her forehead.

He turned and saw me. "Bea – I heard about Ronnie…"

We ended up, the three of us, sitting in that loosebox while I told my tale.

"Best thing to happen," he said at the end.

"Your leg…" I began

"I'm managing well – I'm to have a false one – when they get around to it. I can do a lot on my crutches anyway."

He sounded cheerful – as if he had almost forgotten the horrors he'd seen and how I'd rebuffed his proposal.

The young filly nuzzled at me, her whiskers brushing my face. "She's just like Star," I said.

"Her sister. And this one – she's only six months – will be too young to go to war. It'll all be over by the time she's broken in."

A stocky girl wearing breeches and an apron came through the door and stopped. "Oh – you've got company, Tod." She smiled at him and her round face lit up so I could see she was attractive in an unusual way. She had curly hair and big brown eyes and Tod gazed at her with a fond look.

Jem winked at me and I chatted a moment, then left with her, happy that Tod had found a girl he could love. "My Da took a while to get used to her but she's strong and always willing – and she loves Tod, leg and all. They'll get wed next Eastertide."

I had a pang of jealousy as I went home. Tod and Sally were only a year or so older than me and yet Ronnie thought me too young.

I cried that night, longing for him. I wanted a letter, not a message sent by his mother.

CHAPTER 28

It was strange, going back to Tanglemere. The dogs remembered me and rushed up, tails wagging. Perse and Herme threw themselves on me and dragged me out to the garden even though the ground was soaked by the rain.

"It's been so boring without you, Miss Denning," Herme said. "Seli's been out nursing and left us with old Maggy – Mrs. Maggs – she's always in a bad temper. After Christmas, we're going to the village school."

I was pleased for them. They would find out how poorer children lived, some still going barefoot to school – and they would enjoy being with others of their own age. But it meant that I wouldn't be needed any more.

It began to rain again, so we went indoors.

I decided I had to be firm and make them work. The village schoolmistress would be quick to rap their hands with a ruler if they romped about.

"Singing, please Miss Denning!" they pleaded.

I always love the big drawing-room, with its big windows on either side and now the sun shafted through the clouds outside as I played the familiar songs, the girls joining in. I added one from *"To-night's the Night"* but the memory of that wonderful week, when I was on a happy cloud of love and song – made me cry as I sang.

"That's lovely – don't cry," Herme said.

Suddenly there was a thump at the window and I looked up to see wing-marks where a bird had hit the glass. We ran outside and I found one of Maggs' doves, lying in the flowerbed. I felt sick. This time it really was an omen. Something would happen to Ronnie and I would never see him again.

Perse crouched down. "It's breathing," she said. "Let's take it indoors, away from the dogs."

I picked it up. This time, there was no blood but the poor bird was half-conscious, its beak open and its white breast fluttering faintly.

I found myself muttering "please don't die," as we found a shoebox, lined with a soft cloth and put the dove inside. Of course the dogs tried to follow us.

"Let's put it in the studio," Herme suggested. "It'll be quiet there."

Reluctantly, because I didn't want to be reminded of Ronnie, we carried the box outside and walked towards the studio. Mr. Maggs appeared, pushing a wheelbarrow and stopped us. "You got one of my doves?"

"It stunned itself on the window," I explained.

"Won't live. They usually die of shock." He touched its back with a dirty but gentle finger. "That's one of my young ones." He sounded sad.

"Please yourself," he said when I asked if we could put it in the studio. "But them girls must know creatures die. 'Ashes to ashes, dust to dust'" he intoned as he went off.

I wished he hadn't said that.

The studio was cold and dust had collected on every surface. There was the portrait, still hanging where Ronnie had left it.

I looked into the face of the child I had been then.

"You going to grow your hair again Miss?" Perse asked.

"I don't think so," I said.

Herme put the box holding the dove on the couch where I'd sat – where Ronnie had kissed me…

"If it revives, it will need a way out," I said.

Perse operated some kind of pulley and opened a skylight

window.

Herme was stroking the dove's head and I had to persuade them to leave the poor creature to its fate.

That evening, I read a story to Jimmy, who one minute seemed his old cheeky self and the next, asked painful questions about Alex's death – had it hurt a lot? Where was he buried? Could we go to the grave? None of them could be answered.

Next morning I waited for the post lady before going to Tanglemere. But there was no letter from Ronnie. Was he trying to cut himself off from me because I was too young to marry or did he think I was just sorry for him, having a disfigured face?

The day was as grey and depressing as my thoughts and as I cycled, I remembered the poor little dove. I was sure it would be dead, like the other two birds who had haunted me. The girls would be upset, I knew. And I felt sure it would mean that Ronnie could slip out of my life for ever.

Of course the girls rushed me off to the studio right away. "Old Maggy made us tidy our rooms and she wouldn't let us go out," Herme complained.

We told the dogs to wait outside and opened the studio door. Herme ran to the box. "It's empty!" she said.

Then I saw a white feather on the couch and a scattering of bird droppings. We looked round but there was no sign of the dove. Herme looked up at the open skylight. "It's flown away! We cured it!" she said.

She and Perse did a wild dance round the studio, knocking brushes and a pot of paint to the floor. I made them help me clear up and then I found a painting Ronnie hadn't finished, propped on an easel but facing the wall.

It was a bleak battlefield scene – a ruined desolate countryside littered with dead and wounded soldiers, some bleeding, some transfixed on barbed wire as if they had been trying to get through. In the foreground was a shell-hole – the

175

perspective was skewed so I could see bits of bodies and a wounded soldier looking upwards, his mouth crying out for help. Some of the oil paint was still tacky under my finger so it must be Ronnie's last picture, painted before he had his Army Medical.

The wounded soldier's face was Ronnie's.

"What are you looking at, Miss Denning?" Perse asked but I turned the picture back to the wall and hurried them out so we could tell Mr. Maggs his dove would be returning.

That evening my mood had changed. I felt sure that the dove's recovery meant Ronnie would be writing to me – perhaps even saying he couldn't live without me.

Even Mother seemed less strained and tearful, quietly planning with Father the service to commemorate Alex's life. Jimmy was in bed and we were having our evening cocoa when there was a knock on the front door which set Bertie off barking and growling.

"Whoever can that be, so late?" Mother asked as I followed her into the little hallway. She lowered her voice "Your father still doesn't know about the broken window and that horrible note about our German connections. They've not been back since we had Bertie."

"Wasn't that a car stopping outside?" I asked. "Those stone-throwers wouldn't have a motor-car."

I opened the door. The gas light in the hall shone on Mrs. Rossiter's face, shiny with tears. "Beatrice – there's been another Zeppelin attack in London, this time in Theatreland – near the Gaiety. Mr Rossiter telephoned me. His – lady-friend – is suffering from shock and they don't know where Ronnie is. Will you come with me to London?"

CHAPTER 29

I was crying so much that Mother agreed I should go but she made me put warm clothes on before I got into Mrs. Rossiter's car. I was glad of them because the hood was as draughty as the one on Bunny's car and it began to rain as we drove up the endless roads to London.

Mrs Rossiter didn't speak but crouched at the wheel, driving the bigger car much faster than her husband. I felt sick, slipping about on the leather seat when the car jolted over holes in the road and swerved dangerously round corners.

After what seemed hours, I saw the familiar blue-tinged London lights and we drove into Red Lion Square. I was surprised that Mrs. Rossiter knew the way but guessed for some reason, perhaps to spy on her rival? – she had been there before.

There was no time to wonder if she would be embarrassed, meeting her husband's mistress because Mr. Rossiter answered the door. To my complete surprise, he hugged his wife to him and she sobbed on his shoulder.

"Come upstairs," he said.

Bunny was sitting in the drawing-room, still in her stage costume and make-up. The two women stared at each other and then Bunny walked shakily over to Selina Rossiter and put out her hand. The next moment, I could hardly believe it as the two women were embracing and crying.

"The bombs fell during the performance – the door to the scene-dock was destroyed and bits of shrapnel fell on the stage but we kept on and the audience stayed in their seats," Bunny's voice shook. "Then when we came out we saw the road outside was in ruins and…" She lowered her voice. "Dead and injured just lying there – people rushing past – a fire-engine…"

Mr. Rossiter went on. "I was watching the show that night. Outside, there was panic and chaos. I told Bunny to wait and I would walk for a cab. I went back into the theatre to tell Ronnie not to go outside yet– he'd been adding up the takings – but he wasn't there. The box office girl was in hysterics because of the bombs – but I got it out of her that Ronnie heard that the theatre's messenger boy and call-boy had gone out just before the bombs fell – on some errand for the Stage Manager – and Ronnie said he'd see if they were safe. I've been trying to ring the Charing Cross hospital but I can't get through."

"We had to walk some distance to find a cab," Bunny said. "We heard an omnibus had been blown up and the rear of another theatre hit. We telephoned you as soon as we got home. Gervaise said we should wait for news but I knew you would want to know."

Selina Rossiter got up. "I'm going to the hospital to see if he's there."

I was trying hard to keep calm but I kept imagining Ronnie buried under a heap of rubble. "I'll come with you."

In the end, all of us got into the car. As we went through Trafalgar Square we could see lights and flares and hear the ringing of ambulance bells away to our left. We had to abandon the car by Charing Cross station because of the ambulances going down the narrow road to the hospital.

I tucked my skirts up and ran for all I was worth, Selina Rossiter close by me and Bunny panting behind us with Gervaise Rossiter.

"Who're you shoving?" said a large man, who was holding a cloth to his bleeding face. "You got to stand in the queue for treatment."

I ignored him, side-stepped and found the same big waiting-room. I ran past the injured and sick waiting on benches and saw the young doctor who had examined Ronnie before, just going into a curtained cubicle. I grabbed his arm. "Please – we're looking for someone." I very nearly gave Ronnie's name. "Joe Hodges. You saw us before."

He gave no sign of recognising me and then I remembered Ronnie was Alan Drummond when he came in. "Ask at the desk, please," he said.

I looked across and saw the Rossiters and Bunny waiting in another queue while a flustered nurse tried to deal with the anxious relatives of the injured.

That would take too long. I tried not to think Ronnie might be dead and ran down the line of cubicles, looking through, seeing injured men and even a woman and child but no Ronnie. Someone was shouting at me but I took no notice and looked through the last cubicle. A man totally covered in grey dust and debris sat near a patient who was moaning and calling out in a thin boy's voice, "Mum, Mum!" as the doctor bent over him.

I saw the boy's black hair and sallow face and recognised as the theatre's cheeky call-boy, Freddy. At the same moment a nurse gripped my shoulder from behind, and the grey man turned his head and looked at me with red-ringed eyes. "Bea!"

I shook off the nurse and ran to him, smothering myself with dust as I hugged him.

Ronnie was unhurt but he didn't want to leave Freddy, whom he'd found half-buried in a hole in the road, clutching the dead hand of the theatre's Messenger-boy.

Mrs. Rossiter used her stiff and bossy manner to get Ronnie out of the hospital and he walked shakily to the motor-car. There wasn't room for us all so Bunny and Gervaise Rossiter said they would try to find a cab.

I insisted on sitting next to him at the back of the car and covered both of us with the travelling rug, holding him in my arms. "Oh Bea – I have missed you," he muttered. "And the bomb attack – it was like the Dolphin again. But I must get back to the theatre and tell them…" then he suddenly fell asleep.

It was like a dream, his head on my shoulder so near I could smell the dust and debris still stiff in his hair. So like a dream that I didn't notice how long it was taking to get to Bunny's house.

"Where are we?" I asked.

"I'm taking him home," Mrs. Rossiter said.

"But he can't…" I began.

"He's Joe Hodges, a young man Ronnie studied with at the Slade," she shouted over the loud noise of the car back-firing. "A friend of yours, Beatrice," she added. "And we can truthfully say he was involved in the latest Zeppelin bombing. As soon as he's recovered, he can go back to the theatre."

I wasn't sure Ronnie would agree but it was so wonderful having him close to me that I didn't care. All the same, there was a danger someone might recognise him, scarred as he was. Would his false identity hold up to Police scrutiny?

CHAPTER 30

I was exhausted when Mrs. Rossiter left me at home. We'd stopped on the way so she could pour more petrol into the engine from a can she carried. Then one of the car lights failed and we had to go slower, so the journey took for ever. It was still dark when we arrived and I had no idea of the time. "Come and see us tomorrow," Mrs. Rossiter said as she drove off.

I was surprised to find Mother already up, having her morning tea.

I told her Ronnie was safe but she wouldn't let me talk any more and bundled me into bed. I tried to drink the cup of hot milk and honey but I kept falling asleep.

When I woke, I heard church bells ringing and realised it was Sunday. I had to see Ronnie. He had been nervous of being recognised in the village and might very well have taken himself back to London on our one Sunday train. But if he really loved me – wouldn't he stay?

Bertie nearly knocked me over when I went downstairs, lovingly licking my face and blowing doggy-breath all over me. I found a note from Mother on the kitchen table saying the porridge was on the stove and they had gone to church – Jimmy was going to pump the organ. "*Please rest, Bea darling,*" she wrote.

I couldn't eat the porridge nor rest. I drank some milk, then scribbled a note to Mother, saying I had gone to Tanglemere.

I cycled as fast as I could through the quiet Sunday village, hardly noticing it was a golden autumn day.

Could I creep round to the studio, without anyone noticing? But the dogs gave me away, barking behind the front door so I had to knock.

Mrs. Rossiter looked pale and distracted when she opened the door. "Oh Beatrice," she said. "The girls are both in bed with fevers and a rash. I'm waiting for the doctor. And the Maggs have the day off to visit their daughter in Lower Mere. Now you're here, Beatrice, could you take Ronnie a tray of breakfast and tell him his father has telephoned – he's heard from the theatre that Freddy, the call-boy, is conscious and recovering."

As I prepared a tray with toast and tea, I couldn't help wishing the Rossiters were church-going folk – then I would be alone with Ronnie.

I found the studio door bolted so I put the tray down and knocked, loudly. Nothing happened. "It's me – Beatrice," I said.

The door was unbolted and Ronnie stood there, wearing a dressing-gown. He looked rumpled and half-asleep. He stared at me strangely.

"I've brought breakfast," I said, biting back tears. He didn't seem glad to see me, after all. Then I told myself not to be a coward. "I'll bring the tray inside," I said firmly. "Your mother asked me – the girls have a fever and she's waiting for the doctor. And your father's telephoned to say Freddy, is conscious and getting better."

"Oh dear, the girls weren't too well when I arrived." He looked worried. "But it's good about young Freddy – I like him and he works hard." He stood back to let me come in.

I put the tray on the littered table and I heard him bolt the door. Then he was just standing there, running his fingers through his bleached hair, which contrasted so with his brown eyes and dark eyebrows. His maimed hand was shaking. "Sorry – but that second bomb attack brought things back," he said.

I put my arms round him and felt his body quiver.

For a moment he just stood quite still and I thought he was going to tell me to go away. He kissed me into silence, wrapping me in love. "Marry me, dearest Bea," he murmered.

I shivered with delight and I tried to say, "I love you," but he kissed me into silence.

My heart thudded. I longed to be with him always but suddenly I felt it was a huge commitment – and I still wanted to go on the stage. "Couldn't we live together, at the theatre?" I asked.

He drew back. "I thought you wanted to marry me. Besides, it would hurt your family if they found out. And supposing you had a baby?"

I felt myself blushing as I said, "Nowadays there are ways of prevention." Violet and the other girls had gone into some detail. Apparently there was a book by someone called Marie Stopes which told you all about sex.

"But you do want children?"

"Of course. But not yet."

We kissed again but didn't dare linger – Mrs. Rossiter might wonder why I was so long.

"Would you come and see my parents?" I asked. "You'll have to ask my father if we can marry. He's old-fashioned, you know." I dreaded this. Father could forbid us to marry until I came of age.

He looked away from me. "Supposing I'm recognised?"

"You won't be. Everyone thinks you're dead and you look – different."

He fingered the ridge of his scar. "Yes. And what do I tell your parents? I can't make you Mrs. Rossiter – you will become Mrs. Hodges."

I was impatient with him. "What does that matter? I want to live with you in London and I don't care what I'm called if I can be with you always. And maybe you can be Ronnie

Rossiter again one day. When the war is over they won't be looking for you."

Still in his dressing-gown, he was arranging his brushes and paints with an abstracted look. "This war – won't stop until thousands more are killed. They'll have conscription next – men and boys will have to enlist."

"Well, they won't make Joe Hodges enlist – I imagine you can't handle a gun with a one hand that doesn't work properly even if you can hold a brush with the other?"

Unconsciously, he curled up his maimed hand. I knew he didn't like me to see it.

"You're tea's gone cold!" I smiled. "Drink it and let's tell your mother we're engaged. Now the doctor's seen the girls we can find out what's wrong with them." I hated to think of that lively, unruly pair having a serious illness.

"I think my mama may have guessed about us," and he put down the cup of cold tea and held me close.

I smiled to myself, thinking how intimate we had been, as he modestly went behind the screen to put on his underwear and the rough wool shirt Joe Hodges would wear. "What about the Maggs?" he called out.

"Off for the day. Nobody will see you."

We walked towards the house but stopped when we saw the doctor's carriage by the house, his chestnut mare tied to a railing. "We can't go in – he thinks I'm dead," Ronnie said.

"Let's go to the rose garden," I suggested.

We walked over the wet grass, where dew-drops glittered like diamonds in the myriad spiders-webs and came to the wrought-iron seat by the rose garden. He took off the rough woollen jacket he'd bought off a London market stall and spread it out on the seat. Then he swept off his flat cap and bowed to me. "Rest here, my Beata Beatrix."

I laughed. "You are indeed courtly, Oberon."

Although bright leaves still clung to the trees, nearly all the roses were dead. Ronnie pushed into the prickly bushes and picked a perfect bloom, giving it to me and saying, "It's the last rose of summer, my love."

I felt sick with memory as I saw drops of blood fall from his maimed hand. "You're bleeding," I said.

He sat down, putting his arm round me. "I've lost much of the sensation in that hand so I never noticed the thorns."

A robin serenaded us with his sweet, high song as we sat in happy silence. Then he said, "I'd like to see Joe's grave – or rather, my own grave." He smiled a little sadly.

"We'll go – after we've seen your mother."

When we walked back we found the doctor's carriage had gone.

Mrs. Rossiter answered the door. "You can't come in," she said. "It's scarlet-fever. It's a blessing I'm a nurse."

Scarlet fever was a serious illness, killing two young children in the village last year. I was fearful for the girls. "Can I see them – and help you?" I asked.

"No, thank you, Beatrice. I don't want either of you to catch it."

"Give them our love," Ronnie said. "And tell us if you need anything." Then he blurted out, "Seli – Mama – we have something to tell you. Beatrice has agreed to marry me. Isn't it wonderful?"

She looked surprised and I waited for her to tell us we were too young. Then she said, "That's wonderful news!" and enveloped us in a cloud of Jeyes Fluid disinfectant as she hugged us.

I cycled ahead through the village, Ronnie following me. I guessed he was nervous. I was almost sure he didn't have to worry because the scar had altered his face which was half-hidden by the flat woollen cap he wore.

The churchyard was empty, except for one very old woman, tending a grave. She didn't look up as we left our cycles and walked between the tombstones.

The new graves were at the far end but of course, Alex

didn't have a grave. Instead, he was to have a plaque in the church dedicated to him.

Ronnie caught up with me. "Here it is," he said. "So strange to see my name. I wonder where I shall be buried when I die a second time."

I didn't like to think of that.

Dying flowers and wreaths were heaped on the grave and the stone-mason had worked quickly on the granite headstone.

Oberon Rossiter, beloved son of Gervaise and Selina b.1897 d.1915.

We stood hand in hand, and I know we were both thinking of poor Joe Hodges, who had given Ronnie the chance of a new life.

Ronnie threw away the dead flowers and I put the single red rose on the grave. I began to cry as I remembered my brother, buried in a foreign field.

Alex's death hadn't seemed real up to now.

For the first time, I knew I would never see him again – unless Heaven existed and I wasn't at all sure that it did.

CHAPTER 31

It was the beginning of December. The winter had brought snow and hard frost to freeze the Drummonds' lake and I stood alone, watching the skaters – young men zooming round, showing off and getting in the way of more sedate couples dancing on skates to the appropriately named Skaters' Waltz. The music came from a gramophone, wound up by the Drummonds' new chauffeur.

The red setting sun tinged the ice blood red and there was an orange glow from the oil lamps and candles surrounding the lake. The Drummonds' cook was roasting chestnuts on the glowing iron brazier, where the older villagers huddled for warmth.

The Drummonds' servants had brought chairs, rugs, mulled wine and mince-pies and many people from Upper and Lower Mere were there, invited to put money, big or small, into collecting boxes brought round by Jimmy and his school friends. The money raised would go towards Christmas comforts for the troops.

Nurses, including Jem, Elizabeth and Mrs. Rossiter, had brought the more able-bodied officers in wheelchairs or by car, slipping and sliding on the half-frozen track to the lake. I was surprised to see how tenderly Elizabeth was tucking a rug round one of the men – I saw him quickly grasp her hand and she didn't pull it away.

Someone pulled Jem away from the wounded men – perhaps it was Ian, the young doctor she'd mentioned to me, very casually. They did a wild dance together – bumping into other couples, nearly falling and I could hear their laughter.

I was at the edge of the ice and now I saw Tod, carefully sliding on his one foot, Sally's arm supporting him round the lake. He staggered and they both laughed. He was still waiting for his false leg, there having been a great demand for limbs for amputees in the last months but he didn't seem to mind, now he had Sally.

Everyone had a partner, and I was alone. Ronnie had promised to come from London, but he was late. Perhaps the train had been held up by the snow. This was the first time he had been back to Upper Mere since we had made love.

I thought of that happy but frustrating time I had in November, when I had gone to London for a week, staying with at the theatrical lodgings with Violet and the girls and helping back-stage. I had to convince the Manager I was useful, not only as a chorus understudy but assisting the dresser and even selling programmes.

Ronnie wouldn't let me stay the night because he said my parents trusted him now. All we managed in the daytime were passionate kisses in Ronnie's dusty room at the theatre, surrounded by props and scenery, and we were often interrupted by a stage-hand. I had to share a room with Violet at the lodgings – and of course she teased me about my 'Joe' but I got on with her better now and absorbed all I could about singing and dancing in the theatre.

My father had found out about the Rossiters' pending divorce and he had only let me stay in London if I promised not to go to Bunny's house nor stay with Ronnie. He was so straight-laced and old-fashioned – but I knew how much Alex's death and the war itself had upset him, so I agreed.

My parents had stayed at home this evening because they still wanted to be quiet, remembering Alex. I thought of my father's expression when Ronnie came to ask if we might marry. At last Father had said, "I don't like the fact you have changed your identity – I never like deception. And Beatrice is still very young."

Mother had touched his sleeve at that point and I held my breath. If he refused, I certainly wouldn't wait until I came of age – I would either live with Ronnie or persuade him to elope.

I knew Mother was on my side but she was a woman of her time, always deferring to a man. If her beloved David refused permission, she would go along with it.

"I will give my permission for you to marry when you are seventeen," Father said. "That will give you time to reflect and Ronnie – Joe – time to make a home for you."

That was far too long to wait!

"But you and Mother," I began, remembering they had eloped.

"I was nearly eighteen," Mother said.

I was almost cross with Ronnie because he just thanked Father, politely and they shook hands. It was all so old-fashioned. I was sure this formality wouldn't be around after the war.

Ronnie reminded me afterwards that we would have to marry in London, just in case he was recognised in the village. He said there was a small but beautiful church in Hampstead, near his father's studio. I didn't care where it was – I just wanted to be with him and to be working in the theatre.

Now Jimmy was screaming with delight as he slid over the ice with the other children, including Perse and Herme. They had been ill for some time but now behaved just as madly as ever – but I was glad for Jimmy's sake – he had been so upset by Alex's death.

I skated on, past the lights and the dancers, to the far end where Ronnie and I had sat on the carved tree-trunk. Stars were coming out and I began to doubt that he would come. He was still so nervous of being recognised.

I slid off the ice, sat on the frozen bank and took off my skates. I would sit and remember that hot summer day and how we kissed. I brushed the snow off the carved seat and sat down. Here, the skaters' shouts and the music were dimmed by the trees.

I thought about Alex and felt guilty again, that I had hated him for his teasing. If only life could roll backwards.

Then – just for a moment – and of course it was a trick of the deepening dusk – I thought I saw my brother, tall and thin, racing down the lake just as he had last winter. Then he was gone into the shadows.

Was that someone calling my name? Again I saw a dark figure, skating towards me, but carefully, not with Alex's skill.

"Bea – is that you?" Ronnie's voice.

"No – I'm a ghost!" I stood up, laughing and happy. "You look like a large gnome, wearing that red woolly bobble hat."

He picked his way up the bank, still on his skates and hugged me close. He smelled of train-soot, of cold air – and of himself.

"Let's sit here." I drew him down to the carved seat.

"This is where we kissed," he said and at once kissed me again, his lips ice-cold on mine.

We took off our gloves and held hands.

"I've been thinking of Alex. I even fancied I saw his ghost, skating," I said. "We're so happy but somehow forgetting the men – and women, I suppose – the nurses and ambulance drivers – who are dying out there, at the Front."

"I don't forget," he said slowly. "Dying in pools of their own blood, drowning in some muddy crater, or slowly, of gangrene in a field hospital. Sometimes I feel guilty. But even if I could use my hand properly – I couldn't go back. I still wake up, screaming with nightmares."

"You won't when I'm with you. We can hold one another."

He was still staring ahead, thinking. "So what's this war about? Gaining a few feet in a muddy field? Is it 'the war to

190

end all wars'? There will be more wars, more dying for the wrong reason. You know the writer Kipling?"

"Of course."

"After his son died this autumn – and he was only 17, Kipling wrote some lines:

"If any question why we died,
Tell them because our fathers lied."

I tried to dispel his black mood. "We're part of the future. We can change things"

I dusted the snow off the Green Lady so I could see the carved words flowing from her mouth. I knew them by heart so I recited, *"Life is good. Live gently, with fire and always with hope.* That's a message for us. The war will end soon. And we shall get married and I shall become a famous actress and you will become a famous painter. Just you wait and see."

He smiled and drew me very close. "I don't know if I can wait until you are seventeen," he said, kissing my cold ear and then scattering butterfly kisses, light as snowflakes, all over my face, so again I was afire with love and longing.

"I read somewhere – *Love conquers all*," I said when I could breathe again.

"I'll agree to that, Bea darling." And his good hand stroked any parts of me he could reach through all our winter clothing.

Then we held each other close, ready to conquer the world.